WHAT'S FOR DINNER?
IN ONE POT

WHEN USING KITCHEN APPLIANCES PLEASE ALWAYS FOLLOW
THE MANUFACTURER'S INSTRUCTIONS

HarperCollins*Publishers*
1 London Bridge Street
London SE1 9GF

www.harpercollins.co.uk

HarperCollins*Publishers*
Macken House, 39/40 Mayor Street Upper
Dublin 1, D01 C9W8, Ireland

First published by HarperCollinsPublishers 2023

1 3 5 7 9 10 8 6 4 2

Text © Sarah Rossi 2023
Photography © Sam Folan 2023

Sarah Rossi asserts the moral right to be identified as the author of this work

A catalogue record of this book is available from the British Library

ISBN 978-0-00-856771-2

Design by Lynnette Eve at Design Jam

Photographer: Sam Folan
Food Stylist: Pippa Leon
Prop Stylist: Rebecca Newport

Printed and bound at GPS Group, Slovenia

FSC
www.fsc.org

MIX
Paper from
responsible sources
FSC™ C007454

This book is produced from independently certified FSC™ paper
to ensure responsible forest management.

For more information visit: www.harpercollins.co.uk/green

Sarah Rossi

WHAT'S
FOR DINNER?
IN ONE POT

100 Delicious Recipes
10 Weekly Meal Plans
In One Pan or Slow Cooker!

HarperCollins*Publishers*

CONTENTS

INTRODUCTION

INTRODUCTION

I've shared recipes online for nearly 10 years now and the feedback I receive is what shapes every idea I come up with. I'm so grateful for an audience online who let me have a peek into their lives, helping me to understand the true impact of the question 'What's for Dinner?' every night.

You've told me about the strain of juggling work, the school run, getting to clubs and helping with homework; that by the time that you need to think about food, there's no mental energy left. Not to mention the fact that many of us are aiming for meals the whole family will eat, with plenty of goodness included.

In this book, I've tried to relieve you from some of that load by cooking complete meals in a single pan. A one-pot meal reduces the thought processes needed to serve up dinner, along with the washing up and the amount of energy we use.

I hope you can open any page in this book and find something that will give you not only a meal that the whole family will eat and enjoy, but also one that makes your life a little simpler in the process.

Sarah

HOW TO USE THIS BOOK

This book includes Meal Plans for 10 weeks. The idea is you select a daily/weekly plan to save the mental load of having to think about what to make for the week ahead. Use the shopping list for your groceries the weekend before, and you're good to go. Of course, you don't have to stick to the meal plans, and you can vary them to suit your own family's tastes.

If you're using the shopping lists don't forget to check your cupboard and fridge to see what you already have before you go shopping.

The recipes in the book are also organised in chapters, split by meal type, so you can cook individual recipes and return to your favourites.

THE RECIPES

Each dinner is made in a single pan.

Every recipe has been written to cater for family-friendly tastes.

No huge ingredient lists.

THE MEAL PLANS

Each week includes
6 dinners (2 per week with sides),
1 weekend breakfast and 1 sweet treat.

There's a handy shopping list for each week showing exactly what you need to buy. The ingredients are colour coded so you can select the meals you want to cook.

Each week includes 1 or 2 meat-free dishes, a good variety of different carbs and proteins.

WHAT IS ONE-POT COOKING?

One-pot cooking is a complete meal, that uses only one cooking dish.

– Wherever possible, cook protein, carbs and vegetables all in the same pan.

– If carbs and vegetables aren't included in the main cooking dish, you should be able to serve with a no-cook side dish (a salad, a bread or, at a push, microwaveable rice!).

It felt important to me that in the cases where vegetables didn't work in the main dish for example (Slow Cooker Braised Beef Tacos on page 118 and Slow Cooker Sticky Ginger Pulled Ham on page 102 I'm looking at you) we came up with a very quick side dish to serve with them that didn't need an additional cooking pot. So, in each weekly meal plan, you'll find two recipes that offer a no-cook side dish alongside the main.

THE BENEFITS OF ONE-POT COOKING ARE HUGE:

Energy saving

Less washing up

The ˋhands off' approach to not juggling various pans can be a total relief

5 TIPS FOR SUCCESS IN THE KITCHEN

I am not sure if these tips are obvious or not, but honestly, they weren't always obvious to me. In listening to the questions I'm asked online every day about recipes, I hope these words can give you a little boost of confidence (should you need it) to delve into this book and make it your own.

1. **Trust your eyes more than you listen to me.** Every recipe in this book has been tested thoroughly but ingredients, ovens and kitchen temperature all make a difference to the end result. So, trust yourself. If something looks a little dry, add a splash more water; if something isn't cooked, give it a little longer in the pan. You've got this.

2. **Taste and season your food with salt and pepper.** Often, if I try something before serving and think it's just missing a little something, a sprinkle of salt is what's needed. When I really embraced this (embarrassingly, not that long ago) it transformed my cooking. (This doesn't apply if you're cooking for very young children and omitting salt.)

3. **Get to know your own oven or slow cooker.** They vary so much with brand and age. If you begin to notice that yours is fierce and everything cooks quickly, note this and remember to always check a recipe towards the end of the cooking time. (See page 18 'The Pots' page.)

4. **Have one good-quality chef's knife that feels comfortable in your hand.** Keep it very sharp. It's much better to spend money on one excellent knife than a whole block of mediocre ones. It will make every single item you chop feel easier.

5. **If you are worried about undercooking or overcooking food** (particularly meat) invest in a good-quality meat thermometer (I like the Thermapen brand). It removes all of the guess work that can lead to dry, overcooked meat and also the worry of having undercooked food.

WHY ONLY SIX DINNERS?

In the meal plans I've included six dinners, rather than seven, a meal for every evening apart from one, just because I think we need to include a little flexibility in our lives and to make the Meal Plans perhaps more achievable for all. (Yes, you can read between the lines here – every time I've ever planned a week's worth of dinners, I've failed to cook them all, then lost my way altogether!) Let's be kind to ourselves. ❤

A few options for dinner number seven:

★ **BAKED POTATOES**
Choose your own favourite topping. The ultimate comfort food!

★ **A MEAL FROM THE FREEZER**
– see page 16 for options.

★ **LEFTOVERS**
From the week – a single recipe or a mixture of dishes.

★ **SUNDAY ROAST**
Choose your favourite, vegetarian or not.

★ **NO-COOK NIGHT**
Cooked meat, bread and salads.

INGREDIENT NOTES

Olive oil: Use basic olive oil for cooking. Don't use extra virgin as it will burn and it's also a waste of money to cook with as you won't be able to taste the flavour.

Garlic granules: These are a dried garlic and a very useful shortcut sometimes. If you can only find garlic powder (a finer ground version) this is almost always fine to use. Don't confuse with garlic salt, which unsurprisingly, is very salty!

Eggs: Unless otherwise stated, these are medium sized.

Butter: Recipes usually state salted or unsalted. I tend to be quite forgiving about this and I wouldn't let not having the right type of butter stop me using a recipe (assuming you don't mind a savoury salt tang in baked goods). Please don't substitute with margarine of any kind though.

Onions/garlic/ginger: I often substitute these for the pre-chopped frozen versions, which are very handy. Unless they are going into a salad or being eaten raw, this substitution almost always works well.

Size of vegetables: Obviously the size of vegetables can vary a lot and sometimes you'll need to use your own judgment. Unless otherwise stated recipes use a medium-sized onion of about 190g in peeled weight. If yours are small, just use more to achieve a similar weight.

STORECUPBOARD ITEMS

Here is a list of the items you'll see regularly in the storecupboard section of the shopping lists in this book, in case you want to stock up. Don't feel you absolutely have to, but this is here if you do want to be super organised.

BASICS

Sea salt and freshly ground black pepper
Sunflower oil
Olive oil
Balsamic vinegar
Tomato purée
Vegetable stock cubes
Chicken stock cubes
Beef stock cubes
Lamb stock cubes
Cornflour

SAUCES & JARS

White wine vinegar
Worcestershire sauce (or Henderson's Relish)
Dark soy sauce (I like reduced salt)
Oyster sauce
Dijon mustard
Wholegrain mustard
Mint sauce (the vinegary type, not jelly)
Green pesto
Mango chutney
Chilli jam
Sweet chilli sauce
Marmite
Raspberry jam
Maple syrup
Runny honey

DRY SPICES

Cajun seasoning*
Fajita seasoning
Ras el hanout spice mix
Chinese 5-spice
Dried chilli flakes
Paprika*
Sweet smoked paprika
Mild chilli powder
Mild curry powder*
Garlic granules*
Onion powder
Dried oregano*
Dried thyme
Dried sage
Dried parsley
Ground cloves
Ground cumin*
Ground coriander
Ground turmeric
Garam masala
Fennel seeds
Bay leaves
Ground cinnamon

* If you don't want to buy
   too many spices,
   start with just these.

BAKING

Vanilla extract
Cocoa powder
Baking powder
Self-raising flour
Plain flour
Icing sugar
Caster sugar
Soft light brown sugar
Soft dark brown sugar

KEY TO RECIPES

These symbols are used throughout the book for quick reference.

 SAUTE PAN

 SLOW COOKER

TRAYBAKE

❄ DUMP BAG

Ⓥ VEGETARIAN

ⓋⒼ VEGAN

FOOD FOR YOUR MOOD

Food for a crowd

These recipes are all easy to double and are hands off enough to allow you time to relax with visitors.

– Slow Cooker Sticky Ginger Pulled Ham *(p.102)*
– Beef & Mushroom Pot Pie *(p.114)*
– Slow Cooker Sweet Potato & Quinoa Chilli *(p.64)*
– Spanish-ish Chicken & Chorizo Rice *(p.154)*
– Slow Cooker Meat-free Monday Tacos *(p.60)*

Throw it all in

These are recipes that need hardly any chopping or attention, for those days when you really can't quite think about dinner.

– Creamy Gnocchi Traybake *(p.76)*
– Salmon Primavera Pasta *(p.88)*
– Slow Cooker Sneaky Veg Mac & Cheese *(p.68)*
– Speedy Ginger Pork Stir-fry *(p.182)*
– Caprese Pasta *(p.94)*

For freezing

All of these recipes are perfect for batch cooking. Double (or triple!) the recipe and freeze the cooked portions for defrosting and reheating later.

– Slow Cooker Pork Chilli *(p.148)*
– Slow Cooker Chorizo & Bean Stew *(p.153)*
– Slow Cooker Braised Beef Tacos *(p.118)*
– Slow Cooker Bacon & Lentil Soup *(p.128)*
– Sausage Puff Pie (freeze the filling before adding the pastry and baking) *(p.106)*

DUMP BAGS ❄

'Dump Bags' (excuse the name) are a method of prepping the raw ingredients for a slow cook and then freezing until you're ready to cook the meal. You then defrost it and DUMP it in the slow cooker (get it?!).

They are useful if you want to do a batch preparation session to get ahead, rather than shopping, peeling and chopping for each individual recipe.

The following recipes don't require any browning or pre-cooking so are perfect for this.

– Slow Cooker Creamy Vegetable Curry (*p.56*)
– Slow Cooker Honey & Mustard Pork (*p.152*)
– Slow Cooker Lamb & Spinach Curry (*p.134*)
– Slow Cooker Moroccan-style Aubergine
  with Apricots (*p.54*)
– Slow Cooker Satay-style Braised Beef (*p.160*)

Only freeze the ingredients listed in the 'slow cook' section of the ingredients list and leave out any liquid to be added in when you cook the recipe.

Dump Bags need to be fully thawed before cooking if they contain meat. Always thaw the bags in the fridge to ensure they defrost safely.

THE POTS

Every recipe in this book is made in one of three pans. Here they are:

SLOW COOKER

A saviour if you're out of the house all day, when used well, a slow cooker can transform humble ingredients into something altogether more impressive.

A slow cooker that has a pot which can also be used on the hob is particularly useful. This means that if a recipe requires something to be browned (fried) before slow cooking, it can all be done in one pan.

All of the slow cooker recipes in this book have been tested in a 3.5-litre slow cooker. If you are using a larger slow cooker, you may need to adjust the cooking time slightly as they can cook more quickly.

Also, be aware that cakes make in a larger slow cooker will almost certainly be a lot shallower – you may even want to double the recipe for these and freeze the leftovers.

Recommended: Morphy Richards 460012 Slow Cooker Sear and Stew, 3.5 Litre 163W.

SAUTÉ PAN

A sauté pan is basically a deep frying pan or shallow, hob-safe casserole pan. Ideally, it should have a lid and also be suitable for use in the oven and under the grill.

This is a hard-working pan in the kitchen, and if you invest in just one good pan, I suggest making it this one as it can serve so many purposes; frying, roasting, casseroles, the list goes on.

It's particularly handy for any dish that we want to cook mainly on the hob and then finish off under the grill (which is often quicker and more energy efficient than cooking in a conventional oven).

Recommended: MasterClass Shallow Casserole Dish with Lid 4L/28cm, Lightweight Cast Aluminium, Induction Hob and Oven Safe.

BAKING TRAY

Sometimes called a baking sheet, or sheet pan, the difference between this and a roasting tin is lower sides. This is the sort of tray you'd bake cookies on.

While a baking tray isn't deep enough to cook a sauce-based meal on, it enables the heat to circulate well around the food cooking on it, allowing it to cook evenly and crisp up well.

As they are usually larger than a roasting tin, we can also normally fit a whole meal for 4 in one tray.

Recommended: Kitchen Craft Large Baking Sheet KC2BK23, 38 x 30.5cm.

WEEK 1: SHOPPING LIST

FRUIT & VEG

4 onions*	●●●●
½ red onion	●
10 garlic cloves*	●●●
500g white potatoes	●
(such as Maris Piper or King Edward)	
500g sweet potatoes	●
200g long-stemmed broccoli	●
3 carrots	●
1 cauliflower	●
400g chestnut mushrooms	●
200g green beans	●
150g baby spinach	●
100g cherry tomatoes	●
½ white cabbage	●
(use the rest for lunchtime salads)	
4 peppers *(including 1 red)*	●●
150g raspberries	●
150g blueberries	●
3 very ripe bananas	●
1 ripe mango	●
300g fresh pineapple	●
(I buy a tub of ready chopped)	
3 lemons	●●●
1 lime	●

MEAT & FISH

4 skinless, boneless chicken breasts	●
(around 650g)	
750g smoked gammon joint	●
500g diced beef	●
500g turkey mince	●
200g smoked salmon	●

FRIDGE/FREEZER

145g unsalted butter	●
160ml semi-skimmed milk	●
75g grated mozzarella cheese	●
100g cream cheese	●
320g ready-rolled shortcrust pastry	●
200g frozen peas	●

EVERYTHING ELSE

8 eggs	●●●
300g dried pasta	●
400g long-grain rice	●●
4 bread rolls/baguettes	●
Naan breads *(to serve with the curry)*	●
1 x 400g tin black beans	●
1x 400g tin green lentils	●
1x 400ml tin reduced fat coconut milk	●
150g korma curry paste	●
150g apricot jam	●
1 litre ginger ale	●
50g flaked almonds	●
100g chewy/hard toffees	●

STORECUPBOARD

Sunflower oil	●●
Olive oil	●●
Worcestershire sauce	●
(or Henderson's Relish)	
Tomato purée	●●
Green pesto	●
Mango chutney	●
Sweet chilli sauce	●
Vegetable stock cubes	●
Chicken stock cubes	●●
Beef stock cubes	●
Dried chilli flakes	●
Fajita seasoning	●
Garlic granules	●
Dried oregano	●
Dried thyme	●
Ground ginger	●
Garam masala	●
Ground cinnamon	●
Plain flour	●●
Self-raising flour	●
Soft light brown sugar	●
Runny honey / Maple syrup	●
Sea salt and freshly ground black pepper	

* Buy frozen if you prefer

MONDAY

Creamy Vegetable Curry (p.56)

TUESDAY

Zesty Chicken Pilaf (p.170)

WEDNESDAY

Salmon Primavera Pasta (p.88)

THURSDAY

Sticky Ginger Pulled Ham (p.102)
Pineapple Crunch Salad (p.113)

FRIDAY

Turkey Taco Rice (p.140)

SATURDAY

Beef & Mushroom Pot Pie (p.114)

BREAKFAST

Dutch Baby (p.46)
Mango Salad (p.46)

TREATS

Banoffee Cake (p.198)

MONDAY

Creamy Gnocchi Traybake *(p.76)*

TUESDAY

Chicken Cacciatore Pasta *(p.74)*

WEDNESDAY

Moroccan-style Aubergine with Apricots *(p.54)*
Feta Couscous *(p.62)*

THURSDAY

Bacon & Lentil Soup *(p.128)*

FRIDAY

Cumin-crusted Lamb Bake *(p.98)*
Cooling Cucumber Salad *(p.112)*

SATURDAY

Salmon with Feta & Orzo *(p.101)*

BREAKFAST

Peanut Butter Granola *(p.32)*

TREATS

Pear & Chocolate Crumble *(p.204)*

WEEK 2: SHOPPING LIST

FRUIT & VEG

- 2 onions*
- 1 red onion
- 5 garlic cloves*
- 1kg white potatoes (such as Maris Piper or King Edward)
- 2 aubergines
- 5 carrots
- 1 cauliflower
- 2 courgettes
- 400g chestnut mushrooms
- 250g baby spinach
- 400g cherry tomatoes
- 8 spring onions
- 1 cucumber
- 750g pears
- 1 lemon
- 2 limes
- 35g fresh basil
- 25g fresh mint

MEAT & FISH

- 650g skinless, boneless chicken breasts
- 4 lamb steaks *(about 600g)*
- 250g smoked bacon
- 200g smoked bacon lardons
- 4 salmon fillets *(about 500g)*

FRIDGE/FREEZER

- 100g unsalted butter
- 200g natural yoghurt
- 165g garlic & herb cream cheese
- 175g Parmesan cheese
- 200g feta cheese
- 1kg frozen butternut squash

EVERYTHING ELSE

- 500g long-life ready-made gnocchi
- 250g dried pasta
- 300g dried orzo
- 320g couscous

- 200g dried red lentils
- 3 x 400g tin chopped tomatoes
- 2 x 400g tin chickpeas
- 80g flaked almonds
- 75g salted peanuts
- 75g milk chocolate chips
- 100g dried apricots
- 150g jumbo oats
- 75g peanut butter
- Crusty bread *(to serve with the soup)*

STORECUPBOARD

- Sunflower oil
- Olive oil
- Tomato purée
- Green pesto
- Vegetable stock cubes
- Ras el hanout spice mix
- Garlic granules
- Ground cumin
- Dried oregano
- Ground coriander
- Dried chilli flakes
- Sweet smoked paprika
- Paprika
- Garam masala
- Ground cinnamon
- Cornflour
- Plain flour
- Caster sugar
- Runny honey
- Sea salt and freshly ground black pepper

* Buy frozen if you prefer

WEEK 3: SHOPPING LIST

FRUIT & VEG

2 onions* ● ●
2 red onions ● ●
10 garlic cloves* ● ● ●
1.25kg white potatoes ●
(such as Maris Piper or King Edward)
1 broccoli ●
550g chestnut mushrooms ● ●
150g sugar snap peas ●
2 carrots ●
½ red cabbage ●
(use the rest for lunchtime salads)
200g cherry tomatoes ●
5 peppers *(at least 3 red)* ● ●
14 spring onions ● ●
4 apples *(if you buy a pack* ●
use the rest as snacks)
100g raspberries ●
2 lemons ●
25g fresh basil ● ●
15g fresh parsley ●

MEAT & FISH

1kg beef brisket ●
650g skinless, boneless chicken breasts ●
500g pork mince *(about 10% fat)* ●
450g pork sausages *(or 8)* ●
50g pepperoni slices ●
200g smoked bacon lardons ●
4 skinless cod fillets *(or other white* ●
fish, fresh or frozen about 500g)

FRIDGE/FREEZER

150ml sour cream ●
125g buffalo mozzarella ●
180g Cheddar cheese ● ●
400g grated mozzarella cheese ● ●
200g fresh salsa ●
(from supermarket dips aisle)
320g ready-rolled shortcrust pastry ●
200g frozen peas ●

EVERYTHING ELSE

5 eggs ● ●
4 large tortilla wraps ●
8 small tortila wraps ●
200g long-grain rice ●
250g dried pasta ●
300g straight to wok noodles ●
320g couscous ●
4 x 400g tin chopped tomatoes ● ● ●
1 x 400g tin black beans ●
1 x 200g tin sweetcorn ●
25g sliced olives *(optional)* ●

STORECUPBOARD

Sunflower oil ● ● ●
Olive oil ● ● ●
Dark soy sauce *(I use reduced salt)*
Oyster sauce
Tomato purée ●
Green pesto
Sweet chilli sauce
Vegetable stock cubes ● ●
Beef stock cubes ●
Chicken stock cubes ●
Fajita seasoning
Chinese 5 spice ●
Mild chilli powder ●
Dried chilli flakes ●
Sweet smoked paprika ●
Garlic granules ● ●
Dried oregano ●
Ground cumin ●
Ground cinnamon ●
Cornflour ●
Caster sugar ●
Runny honey ● ●
Sea salt and freshly ground black pepper

* Buy frozen if you prefer

MONDAY

Nacho Loaded Fries
(p.66)

TUESDAY

Meat Feast Pizza Pasta *(p.84)*

WEDNESDAY

Braised Beef Tacos
(p.118)
Red Slaw *(p.112)*

THURSDAY

Sticky Pork Meatballs
(p.110)

FRIDAY

Hot-headed Cod
(p.132)
Lemon Couscous *(p.146)*

SATURDAY

Pollo Pesto Rice *(p.178)*

BREAKFAST

Easy Cheesy Breakfast Burritos
(p.42)

TREATS

Lazy Fruit Pie *(p.200)*

MONDAY

Paneer Tikka
One-pot (p.52)

TUESDAY

One-pan Rigatoni (p.66)

WEDNESDAY

Italian-style Braised
Beef with Orzo (p.92)
Gremolata (p.92)

THURSDAY

Pork Lettuce
Cups (p.144)
Peanut Dipping Sauce (p.146)

FRIDAY

Fisherman's Bake
(p.120)

SATURDAY

Roasted Oregano &
Lemon Chicken Wraps
(p.104)

BREAKFAST

Cheese & Bacon
Strata (p.38)

TREATS

Double Chocolate
Fudge (p.202)

WEEK 4: SHOPPING LIST

FRUIT & VEG

- 1 onion*
- 2 ½ red onions
- 11 garlic cloves
- 1 tbsp ginger purée*
- 750g white potatoes
  (such as Maris Piper or King Edward)
- 1kg new potatoes
- 1 cauliflower
- 1 broccoli
- 500g chestnut mushrooms
- 1 cucumber
- 450g cherry tomatoes
- 2 salad tomatoes
- 2 or 3 small lettuces (I like little gem)
- 12 spring onions
- 4 lemons
- 10g fresh mint
- 30g fresh parsley

MEAT & FISH

- 500g pork mince (5% fat)
- 400g diced beef
- 4 skinless, boneless chicken breasts
  (around 650g)
- 200g smoked bacon
- 450g pork sausages (or 8)
- 320g fish pie mix (fresh or frozen)
- 150g raw peeled prawns
  (fresh or frozen)

FRIDGE/FREEZER

- 50g salted butter
- 1 litre milk (semi skimmed or full-fat)
- 125g Greek yoghurt
- 300ml crème fraiche
- 250g paneer cheese
- 100g Cheddar cheese
- 75g Parmesan cheese
- 400g frozen peas

EVERYTHING ELSE

- 4 eggs
- 200g bread (preferably stale)
- 400/500g ready-made gnocchi
- 200g dried orzo
- 2 x 250g microwave rice pouches
- 200g long-grain rice
- 4 large flatbreads (or wraps/naans)
- 1½ kg passata
- 1 x 400g tin chopped tomatoes
- 1 x 400g tin chickpeas
- 1 x 225g tin water chestnuts
- 150g tikka masala paste
- 1 x 397g tin condensed milk
- 400g milk chocolate
- 200g white chocolate
- 80g smooth peanut butter
- 150g dried breadcrumbs
  (I like panko)

STORECUPBOARD

- Sunflower oil
- Olive oil
- Balsamic vinegar
- Dark soy sauce (I use reduced salt)
- Oyster sauce
- Sweet chilli sauce
- Vegetable stock cubes
- Beef stock cubes
- Chinese 5 spice
- Sweet smoked paprika
- Dried oregano
- Dried parsley
- Dried thyme
- Garlic granules
- Dried chilli flakes
- Fennel seeds
- Cornflour
- Vanilla extract
- Runny honey
- Sea salt and freshly ground black pepper

* Buy frozen if you prefer

23

WEEK 5: SHOPPING LIST

FRUIT & VEG

2 onions*
3 red onions
8 garlic cloves*
1kg sweet potatoes
500g new potatoes
5 carrots
2 leeks
3 celery sticks
1 avocado
100g cherry tomatoes
3 red peppers
4 sweetcorn cobettes
1 lettuce (*I like cos or romaine*)
2 lemons

MEAT & FISH

500g beef mince (*5% fat*)
1550g skinless,
boneless chicken thighs
450g pork sausages (*or 8*)
200g chorizo (*the type in a ring*)
100g smoked bacon lardons

FRIDGE/FREEZER

100g Salted butter
400g Greek yoghurt (*full fat*)
200g feta cheese
250g ricotta cheese
250g grated mozzarella cheese
80g Parmesan cheese (*grated*)
100g mayonnaise
125g chocolate hazelnut spread
320g ready-rolled puff pastry
200g frozen peas

EVERYTHING ELSE

2 eggs
8 small flour tortillas
250g dried lasagne sheets
200g long-grain rice

150g passata
4 x 400g tin chopped tomatoes
2 x 400g tin green lentils
1 x 400g tin cannellini beans
100g tinned sweetcorn
50g croutons (*optional*)
100g walnuts
30g hazelnuts
50g pecan nuts
125g jumbo oats

STORECUPBOARD

Sunflower oil
Tomato ketchup
White wine vinegar
Worcestershire sauce
(*or Henderson's Relish*)
Tomato purée
Dijon mustard
Marmite
Green pesto
Beef stock cubes
Chicken stock cubes
Paprika
Sweet smoked paprika
Garlic granules
Dried oregano
Bay leaves
Ground cumin
Ground cinnamon
Self-raising flour
Plain flour
Soft dark brown sugar
Caster sugar
Maple syrup
Sea salt and freshly ground black pepper

* Buy frozen if you prefer

MONDAY

Meat-free Monday Tacos (p.60)
Pink Onions (p.62)

TUESDAY

Chicken Stew with Parmesan Dumplings (p.130)

WEDNESDAY

Traffic-light Pizza (p.172)
Caesar-ish Salad (p.174)

THURSDAY

Spanish-ish Chicken & Chorizo Rice (p.154)

FRIDAY

BBQ Sausage & Bean Bake (p.136)

SATURDAY

One-pan Lasagne (p.82)

BREAKFAST

Maple Pecan Granola (p.35)

TREATS

Choco-nut Pinwheels (p.192)

MONDAY

Choosy Bean Tortilla Rolls (p.180)
Speedy Avocado Salsa (p.174)

TUESDAY

Pesto Roast Pork (p.100)

WEDNESDAY

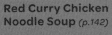

Red Curry Chicken Noodle Soup (p.142)

THURSDAY

Fancy Fish Finger Sandwiches (p.168)
Minted Pea Salad (p.175)

FRIDAY

Creamy Broccoli & Beef Tortellini (p.90)

SATURDAY

Speedy Ginger Pork Stir-fry (p.102)

BREAKFAST

Chorizo Hash Traybake (p.40)

TREATS

Raspberry Bakewell Cake (p.206)

WEEK 6: SHOPPING LIST

FRUIT & VEG

- 2½ red onions
- 9 garlic cloves*
- 10 tsp ginger purée*
- 1.5kg white potatoes (such as Maris Piper or King Edward)
- 4 baking potatoes
- 200g chestnut mushrooms
- 160g sugar snap peas
- 1 broccoli
- 200g green beans
- 200g baby corn
- 2 avocados
- 450g cherry tomatoes
- 2 little gem lettuces
- 3 limes
- 2 lemons
- 15g fresh mint

MEAT & FISH

- 500g pork mince
- 1 pork fillet (also known as tenderloin, about 500g)
- 500g beef mince (5 or 10% fat)
- 300g skinless boneless chicken breasts (or a pack of 2)
- 400g cod fillets, skinless (or other white fish fresh or frozen)
- 200g chorizo (the type in a ring)
- 90g prosciutto slices

FRIDGE/FREEZER

- 195g unsalted butter
- 875ml milk (semi skimmed or full-fat)
- 50g Greek yoghurt
- 4 slices of Cheddar cheese
- 100g feta cheese (optional)
- 250g grated mozzarella cheese
- 50g Parmesan cheese
- 110g mayonnaise
- 2 x 200g fresh tomato salsa (from the supermarket dips aisle)
- 500g frozen peas

EVERYTHING ELSE

- 8 eggs
- 400g dried medium egg noodles
- 2 x 250g microwave rice pouches
- 500g dried tortellini (usually 2 x 250g packs)
- 8 wholegrain tortilla wraps
- 4 burger buns (I like brioche)
- 1 x 400g tin cannellini beans
- 1 x 400g tin black beans
- 1 x 200g tin sweetcorn
- 1 x 400ml tin reduced fat coconut milk
- 2 tbsp Thai red curry paste
- 2 gherkins
- 75g dried breadcrumbs (I like panko)
- 75g ground almonds
- 25g flaked almonds (optional)
- 75g cashew nuts
- 75g smooth peanut butter

STORECUPBOARD

- Sunflower oil
- Olive oil
- Chilli Oil (optional)
- Oyster sauce
- Dark soy sauce (I use reduced salt)
- Green pesto
- Vegetable stock cubes
- Chinese 5 spice
- Fajita seasoning
- Dried chilli flakes
- Dried oregano
- Garlic granules
- Dried parsley
- Plain flour
- Self-raising flour
- Caster sugar
- Runny honey
- Raspberry Jam
- Sea salt and freshly ground black pepper

Buy frozen if you prefer

WEEK 7: SHOPPING LIST

FRUIT & VEG

3 onions* ● ● ●
2 ½ red onions ● ●
14 garlic cloves* ● ● ● ●
750g white potatoes ●
(such as Maris Piper or King Edward)
750g new potatoes ●
2 courgettes ●
200g long-stemmed broccoli ●
4 carrots ●
500g cherry tomatoes ● ●
2 red peppers ●
200g baby corn ●
8 plums ●
1 orange ●
3 limes ● ●
2 lemons ● ●

MEAT & FISH

1.5kg pork shoulder ●
900g skinless, boneless chicken thighs ●
500g beef mince *(5% fat)* ●
600g diced lamb ●
300g frozen raw peeled king prawns ●

FRIDGE/FREEZER

120g unsalted butter ●
150ml milk *(semi-skimmed or full-fat)* ●
400g Greek yoghurt ●
200g garlic and herb cream cheese ●
125g buffalo mozzarella ●
100g feta cheese ●
200g frozen spinach ●
200g frozen peas ●

EVERYTHING ELSE

3 eggs ●
300g dried pasta ●
200g long-grain rice ●
250g dried orzo ●

500g passata ●
1 x 400g tin chopped tomatoes ●
1 x 400g tin black beans ●
1 x 325g tin sweetcorn ●
1 x 400ml tin reduced fat coconut milk ●
3 tbsp Thai red curry paste ●
100g white chocolate chips ●
75g granola ●
Microwave rice, wraps or nachos ●
(to serve with chilli)

STORECUPBOARD

Sunflower oil ●
Olive oil ● ● ● ●
Balsamic vinegar ●
Worcestershire sauce ●
(or Henderson's Relish)
Tomato purée ● ●
Green pesto ●
Mint sauce ●
(the vinegary type, not jelly)
Vegetable stock cubes ● ● ●
Lamb stock cubes ●
Paprika ●
Dried chilli flakes ●
Mild chilli powder ●
Garlic granules ● ●
Dried oregano ● ●
Ground cumin ●
Ground cinnamon ●
Vanilla extract ● ●
Soft light brown sugar ●
Soft dark brown sugar ●
Cocoa powder ●
Baking powder ●
Self-raising flour ●
Plain flour ●
Runny honey ●
Sea salt and freshly ground black pepper ●

* Buy frozen if you prefer

MONDAY

Caprese Pasta *(p.94)*

TUESDAY

Pork Chilli *(p.148)*
Spicy Corn Salad *(p.148)*

WEDNESDAY

Chicken & Feta Traybake *(p.108)*

THURSDAY

Thai-style Red Rice *(p.164)*

FRIDAY

Prawn & Pea Orzo *(p.166)*

SATURDAY

Minted Lamb Stew *(p.138)*

BREAKFAST

Roasted Honey-glazed Plums *(p.44)*
Honeyed Yoghurt *(p.44)*

TREATS

Chocolate Puddle Pudding *(p.188)*

MONDAY

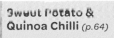

Sweet Potato & Quinoa Chilli *(p.64)*

TUESDAY

Cajun-style Prawn Traybake *(p.116)*

WEDNESDAY

Satay-style Braised Beef *(p.160)*

THURSDAY

Spiced Roast Chicken *(p.156)*
Coronation Couscous *(p.147)*

FRIDAY

Honey & Mustard Pork *(p.152)*

SATURDAY

Crispy Butternut Squash & Feta Pie *(p.58)*
Jewelled Salad *(p.97)*

BREAKFAST

One-pan Pancakes *(p.36)*

TREATS

Kitchen Sink Popcorn *(p.196)*

WEEK 8: SHOPPING LIST

FRUIT & VEG

- 1 onion*
- 3 red onions
- 10 garlic cloves*
- 1 tbsp ginger purée
- 750g sweet potatoes
- 750g new potatoes
- 250g chestnut mushrooms
- 3 carrots
- 3 leeks
- 4 celery sticks
- 200g cherry tomatoes
- 3 green peppers
- 6 spring onions
- 250g vacuum-packed cooked beetroot *(from the fridge)*
- 80g pomegranate seeds
- 150g blueberries
- 250g ripe mango *(I buy a tub of ready chopped)*
- 2 apples
- 1 lemon
- 5g fresh mint

MEAT & FISH

- 700g diced beef
- 1 whole chicken *(approx 1.5kg)*
- 1 pork fillet *(also known as tenderloin, about 500g)*
- 360g raw peeled king prawns *(fresh or frozen)*

FRIDGE/FREEZER

- 350ml milk *(semi skimmed or full-fat)*
- 150ml sour cream
- 100g feta cheese
- 270g filo pastry
- 500g frozen butternut squash
- 150g frozen peas

EVERYTHING ELSE

- 1 egg
- 150g quinoa
- 320g couscous
- 2 x 250g pouches microwave rice
- 500g passata

- 1 x 400g tin chopped tomatoes
- 1 x 400g tin black beans
- 1 x 400g tin chickpeas
- 1 x 325g tin sweetcorn
- 1 x 400ml tin reduced-fat coconut milk
- 60g pine nuts
- 50g flaked almonds *(toasted if possible)*
- 50g peanut butter *(crunchy or smooth)*
- 200g Smarties or M&Ms
- 175g salted peanuts
- 100g tortilla chips
- 100g mini marshmallows
- 200g milk chocolate
- 100g popcorn kernels
- Flatbreads or microwave rice *(to serve with the beef satay)*

STORECUPBOARD

- Sunflower oil
- Olive oil
- Balsamic vinegar
- White wine vinegar
- Dark soy sauce *(I use reduced salt)*
- Tomato purée
- Wholegrain mustard
- Vegetable stock cubes
- Ras el hanout spice mix
- Cajun seasoning
- Paprika
- Mild chilli powder
- Mild curry powder
- Ground cumin
- Garlic granules
- Ground coriander
- Ground turmeric
- Dried parsley
- Vanilla extract
- Baking powder
- Self-raising flour
- Plain flour
- Cornflour
- Soft light brown sugar
- Maple syrup *(to serve with pancakes)*
- Runny honey
- Sea salt and freshly ground black pepper

* Buy frozen if you prefer

WEEK 9: SHOPPING LIST

FRUIT & VEG

5 onions*	●●●●
3 red onions	●●●
7 garlic cloves*	●●
600g white potatoes	●
(such as Maris Piper or King Edward)	
500g new potatoes	●
4 carrots	●
400g chestnut mushrooms	●
200g cherry tomatoes	●
6 salad tomatoes	●●
3 peppers *(whichever colour you prefer)*	●
1 avocado	●
1 lettuce *(I like cos or romaine)*	●
½ cucumber	●
1 lime	●
1 lemon	●
10g fresh mint	●

MEAT & FISH

200g Chorizo *(the type in a ring)*	●
300g skinless, boneless chicken breasts	●
(or a pack of 2)	
450g diced lamb	●
450g pork sausages *(or 8)*	●

FRIDGE/FREEZER

160g unsalted butter	●●
225ml sour cream	●●
75g Parmesan cheese	●
50g Cheddar cheese	●
225g halloumi	●
320g ready-rolled puff pastry	●
400g frozen peas	●●
450g frozen spinach	●

EVERYTHING ELSE

10 eggs	●●●●
300g dried orzo	●
2 x 250g microwave rice pouches	●
500g passata	●

2 x 400g tin chopped tomatoes	●●
1 x 400g tin black beans	●
1 x 400g tin chickpeas	●
1x 325g tin sweetcorn	●
60g salted peanuts	●
100g tortilla chips	●
150g jalfrezi curry paste	●
2 tbsp redcurrant jelly	●
50g white chocolate chips	●
50g dried cherries	●
125g jumbo oats	●
100g crunchy peanut butter	●
Naan or roti *(to serve with the lamb curry)*	●

STORECUPBOARD

Sunflower oil	●●
Olive oil	●●
White wine vinegar	●●
Mango chutney	●
Marmite	●
Vegetable stock cubes	●
Chicken stock cubes	●
Lamb stock cubes	●
Beef stock cubes	●
Fajita seasoning	●
Garlic granules	●
Mild chilli powder	●
Ground cumin	●
Dried oregano	●
Dried sage	●
Dried thyme	●
Bay leaves	●
Garam masala	●
Ground cinnamon	●
Plain flour	●●
Soft light brown sugar	●
Runny honey	●
Sea salt and freshly ground black pepper	

* Buy frozen if you prefer

MONDAY

Mushroom Orzotto *(p.86)*

TUESDAY

Smoky Red Frittata *(p.158)*
Spoonful Salad *(p.147)*

WEDNESDAY

Halloumi Fajita-style Traybake *(p.70)*

THURSDAY

Lamb & Spinach Curry *(p.134)*
Tomato & Onion Salad *(p.134)*

FRIDAY

Chicken Taco Soup *(p.126)*

SATURDAY

Sausage Puff Pie *(p.106)*

BREAKFAST

Chocolate Cherry Granola *(p.34)*

TREATS

Peanut Butter Blondies *(p.190)*

MONDAY

Spanakopita-style Pasta *(p.78)*

TUESDAY

Chicken Tikka-style Traybake *(p.122)*

WEDNESDAY

Chorizo & Bean Stew *(p.153)*

THURSDAY

Sneaky Veg Mac & Cheese *(p.68)*

FRIDAY

Turkey & Lime Burgers *(p.176)*
Sesame & Ginger Slaw *(p.176)*

SATURDAY

Upside-down Loaded Nachos *(p.130)*

BREAKFAST

Yoghurt Breakfast Bark *(p.48)*

TREATS

Pain au Chocolat Bread & Butter Pudding *(p.194)*
Vanilla Crème Fraîche *(p.194)*

WEEK 10: SHOPPING LIST

FRUIT & VEG

- 2 onions*
- 2 red onions
- 2 garlic cloves*
- 1 tsp ginger purée*
- 2 carrots
- 200g long-stemmed broccoli
- 240g baby spinach
- ½ white cabbage *(use the rest for lunchtime salads)*
- 6 salad tomatoes
- 6 peppers *(at least 2 red and 1 green)*
- 2 little gem lettuces
- 200g raspberries
- 200g blueberries
- 1 lemon
- 2 limes
- 10g fresh mint

MEAT & FISH

- 900g skinless, boneless chicken thighs
- 500g turkey mince
- 500g beef mince *(5% fat)*
- 200g chorizo *(the type in a ring)*

FRIDGE/FREEZER

- 30g unsalted butter
- 500ml milk *(semi skimmed or full-fat)*
- 150ml double cream
- 200ml crème fraiche
- 200g cream cheese
- 760g Greek yoghurt *(at least 500g full fat)*
- 100g grated mozzarella cheese
- 100g feta cheese
- 250g mature Cheddar cheese
- 60g mayonnaise
- 500g frozen butternut squash

EVERYTHING ELSE

- 5 eggs
- 4 burgers buns *(such as brioche)*
- 2 x 250g pouches microwavable rice

- 300g dried pasta
- 300g dried macaroni
- 150g long grain rice
- 4 x 400g tin chopped tomatoes
- 1 x 400g tin red kidney beans
- 1 x 400g tin butter beans
- 1 x 400g tin chickpeas
- 1x 400g tin cannellini beans
- 150g tikka masala curry paste
- 30g dried breadcrumbs *(I like panko)*
- 100g tortilla chips
- 2 tbsp white sesame seeds
- 300g pain au chocolat
- 150g granola
- Crusty bread *(to serve with the Chorizo stew)*

STORECUPBOARD

- Olive oil
- White wine vinegar
- Worcestershire sauce *(or Henderson's Relish)*
- Tomato purée
- Wholegrain mustard
- Dijon mustard
- Chilli jam
- Mint sauce *(the naughty type, not jelly)*
- Vegetable stock cubes
- Beef stock cubes
- Paprika
- Sweet smoked paprika
- Mild chilli powder
- Garlic granules
- Onion powder
- Dried oregano
- Ground cumin
- Ground cinnamon
- Vanilla extract
- Icing sugar
- Soft light brown sugar
- Soft dark brown sugar
- Runny honey
- Sea salt and freshly ground black pepper

* Buy frozen if you prefer

WEEKEND BREAKFASTS

SLOW COOKER
PEANUT BUTTER GRANOLA

This isn't a very chunky granola, but I'm willing to forgive that as it's so ridiculously easy and also tastes heavenly. The recipe below serves four, but I'd urge you to consider making a double batch as it keeps well. What a treat to discover this as an easy, ready-made breakfast the following week. Serve with yoghurt and fresh fruit.

SERVES 4

For the Slow Cook
75g peanut butter (smooth works best, but crunchy will work too if it's all you have)
3 tbsp runny honey
125g jumbo oats
75g salted peanuts

To Finish
25g milk chocolate chips

1. Switch the slow cooker on to HIGH. Add the peanut butter and honey and put the lid on, but slightly ajar, for 15 minutes until the peanut butter has softened. Mix with the honey until smooth. (If your peanut butter is particularly runny, you can skip this step.)

2. Add the oats and peanuts and stir everything well until it forms a clumpy mixture. Put the lid on, but again slightly ajar to let the moisture out. Stir it gently just to check it's not sticking after 45 minutes. It will take 1½–2½ hours to cook. Stop it cooking when it's just starting to get crunchy (it won't be fully crunchy, only around the edges, the rest will 'crunch' as it cools).

3. Tip it out onto a baking tray or sheet of baking paper to let it cool and harden.

4. When it's cold, stir in the chocolate chips and store in an airtight container. It will keep in a cupboard for a couple of weeks.

The cooking time can vary a lot depending on which slow cooker you're using (particularly which size it is). Just stir everything occasionally, keep an eye on it and bring it out when it just starts to look cooked.

IF YOU DON'T HAVE A SLOW COOKER...
Cook the 'slow cook' ingredients on a baking tray in a 160°C fan/180°C/Gas Mark 4 oven for 15 minutes, gently stir, then bake for 10–15 minutes until golden. Continue with step 4 above.

CHOCOLATE CHERRY
GRANOLA
p.34

PEANUT BUTTER GRANOLA

MAPLE PECAN GRANOLA
p.35

SLOW COOKER
CHOCOLATE CHERRY GRANOLA

I got a taste for this granola flavour combination after accidentally buying a very expensive shop version. I have come up with this much more affordable granola to make at home which is every bit as delicious. The cooking time can vary a lot depending on which slow cooker you're using (particularly which size it is). Just stir occasionally, keep an eye on it and bring it out when it just starts to look cooked.

1. In a very clean bowl, whisk the egg white until light and fluffy, but not stiff.

2. Mix in all of the other ingredients until well coated.

3. Tip into the slow cooker and cook on HIGH. Leave the lid on, but slightly ajar to let the moisture out.

4. After 1 hour, stir it gently just to check it's not sticking. It will take 1½–2½ hours to cook. Stop it cooking when it's just starting to get crunchy (it won't be fully crunchy, only around the edges, the rest will 'crunch' as it cools.)

5. Tip it out onto a baking tray or sheet of baking paper to let it cool and harden.

6. When it's cool, add the chocolate and cherries. Stir through and serve.

SERVES 4

For the Slow Cook
1 egg white
125g jumbo oats
3 tbsp runny honey
½ tsp ground cinnamon

To Finish
50g white chocolate chips
50g dried cherries

I'd urge you to make double the quantity above as it keeps well in an airtight container in the cupboard for a couple of weeks.

IF YOU DON'T HAVE A SLOW COOKER...
Cook the 'slow cook' ingredients on a baking tray in a 160°C fan/180°C/Gas Mark 4 oven for 15 minutes, gently stir, then bake for 10–15 minutes until golden. Continue with step 6 above.

SLOW COOKER
MAPLE PECAN GRANOLA

1 HOUR 35 MINS, PLUS COOLING TIME

This classic flavour combination makes a deliciously moreish granola. Try to use pure maple syrup rather than a flavoured syrup as the taste is so much better. This granola works particularly well with the Roasted Honey-glazed Plums on page 44.

SERVES 4

For the Slow Cook
1 egg white
125g jumbo oats
3 tbsp maple syrup
50g pecan nuts, roughly chopped
½ tsp ground cinnamon

1. **In a very clean bowl, whisk the egg white until light and fluffy, but not stiff.**

2. **Mix in all of the other ingredients until well coated.**

3. **Tip into the slow cooker and cook on HIGH. Leave the lid on, but slightly ajar to let the moisture out.**

4. **After 1 hour, stir it gently just to check it's not sticking. It will take 1½–2½ hours to cook. Stop it cooking when it's just starting to get crunchy (it won't be fully crunchy, only around the edges, the rest will 'crunch' as it cools.)**

5. **Tip it out onto a baking tray or sheet of baking paper to let it cool and harden.**

The cooking time can vary a lot depending on which slow cooker you're using (particularly which size it is). Just stir everything occasionally, keep an eye on it and bring it out when it just starts to look cooked.

IF YOU DON'T HAVE A SLOW COOKER...

Cook everything on a baking tray in a 160°C fan/180°C/Gas Mark 4 oven for 15 minutes, gently stir, then bake for a further 10–15 minutes until golden.

ONE-PAN PANCAKES

25 MINS

My search for the perfect pancake has been a lifelong one, and I think I perfected them in my first book (after about 200 batches!), but what about those weekends when we can't quite summon the energy to stand by a frying pan? Meet my One-pan Pancakes! Be sure to take these out of the oven when they are just cooked through. It's tempting to cook them until they are golden like traditional pancakes, but the texture is the best when they are still a little pale.

1. Preheat the oven to 180°C fan/200°C/Gas Mark 6.

2. Cut a sheet of baking paper (not greaseproof paper) large enough to cover the base and sides of a baking tray, then press it into the edges of the tin so it sits neatly. Grease the surface of the paper with some oil (I use kitchen paper just to wipe a little oil all over the surface).

3. In a large bowl mix the flour, baking powder and light brown sugar.

4. In a jug, whisk the milk, egg, vanilla and sunflower oil until completely combined.

5. Pour half of the milk mixture into the bowl of flour and whisk until smooth. Add the rest of the milk mixture and whisk until smooth.

6. Pour into the prepared tray and sprinkle over the blueberries. Bake in the oven for 15–20 minutes until cooked through.

7. Remove from the oven, cut into 16 squares and drizzle with maple syrup.

SERVES 4

200g self-raising flour
1 tsp baking powder
40g soft light brown sugar
250ml milk (semi-skimmed or full-fat)
1 egg
1 tbsp vanilla extract
2 tbsp sunflower oil, plus extra for greasing
150g blueberries (fresh or frozen are fine)

To Serve
maple syrup

CHEESE & BACON STRATA

40 MINS

This is a brilliant make-ahead breakfast or brunch dish. It's something like a bread omelette. Perhaps I'm not quite selling it to you there. It's a pan full of cheesy, bacon-studded carbs. Better?! It also happens to be a perfect way to use up stale bread. I love to serve this recipe as part of a breakfast buffet for a crowd.

1. Preheat the oven to 180°C fan/200°C/Gas Mark 6.

2. Put a sauté pan over a high heat and add the bacon pieces (you shouldn't need any oil as they usually have plenty of fat – if yours don't, add 1 teaspoon sunflower oil to the pan). Cook for 5–10 minutes until brown all over.

3. While the bacon is cooking, whisk together the milk, eggs and plenty of salt and pepper until combined.

4. When the bacon is crispy and golden, switch off the heat under the pan and add the bread cubes, tomatoes and spring onions. Give everything a good stir so that the bread is coated in the bacon fat. Pour over the milk and egg mixture and sprinkle the cheese on top.

5. Bake for 30–40 minutes until golden on top and just set (with just a tiny wobble left!).

SERVES 4

200g smoked bacon,
cut into small pieces
500ml milk (semi-skimmed
or full-fat)
4 eggs
300g bread, cut into 3cm cubes
(preferably stale)
250g cherry tomatoes
6 spring onions, cut into 1cm pieces
100g Cheddar cheese, grated
sea salt and freshly ground
black pepper

Stale bread works best here. Save any you have, even if it's very hard.

This is a brilliant recipe to prep in advance, prepare up to step 4, cover and store in the fridge overnight. Bake the next morning for breakfast. (It may need a little longer cooking time if it's chilled.)

Make this vegetarian by leaving out the bacon and step 2 above.

CHORIZO HASH TRAYBAKE

1 HR 10 MINS

This easy little gem of a recipe is here hiding in the Breakfasts chapter, but it would equally make a tasty lunch or dinner. As the chunks of chorizo cook, they flavour the potatoes, zero effort or attention required – just what we love in a meal! We have an egg each, but of course you could add more if you like.

1.25kg white potatoes, such as Maris Piper or King Edward, cut into 2cm cubes (no need to peel)
1 red onion, peeled and cut into wedges
200g chorizo (the type in a ring), cut into 1cm-thick slices
300g cherry tomatoes, halved
4 eggs
sea salt and freshly ground black pepper

1. Preheat the oven to 200°C fan/220°C/Gas Mark 7.

2. Put your potatoes, onion and chorizo on a baking tray and season with salt and pepper. Put into the oven for 45 minutes.

3. About halfway through cooking, give the tray a good shake and shuffle everything about so that the oil being released from the chorizo coats the potatoes.

4. After 45 minutes, when the potatoes are softened, remove the tray from the oven, add the tomatoes and stir so it's all combined.

5. Turn the oven temperature down to 180°C fan/200°C/Gas Mark 6. Using your spatula, make 4 spaces on the tray for the eggs and break an egg into each one. Very carefully return the tray to the oven and cook for a further 12–15 minutes or until the eggs are cooked to your liking.

EASY CHEESY BREAKFAST BURRITOS

25 MINS

A breakfast burrito is infinitely adaptable and utterly satisfying. For me they always need to include eggs and cheese, but you do you. Swap in crispy bacon bits or leftover veggies that need using up.Fried peppers and tinned sweetcorn work well here too. I serve them with a bottle of chilli sauce for drizzling on each bite. You could include some within the wrap before cooking if you prefer a more civilised dining experience.

SERVES 4

2 tsp sunflower oil
450g pork sausages (or 8 sausages)
4 eggs, beaten
4 large tortilla wraps
200g cherry tomatoes, halved
100g Cheddar cheese, grated
sea salt and freshly ground
    black pepper

1. **Heat HALF of the oil in a sauté pan over a medium heat. Add the sausages, squeezing the meat out of the skins into the pan. (I know this is a messy job, but it means they cook into crunchy little pieces. Cut the skins of the sausages lengthways with a knife to help if you like.)**

2. **Using a wooden spoon, break up the sausages and cook for 10 minutes, until browned. Move the sausages occasionally to stop them sticking to the bottom of the pan, but not too much or they will take longer to brown – the sausages should be in small pieces (a bit like mince) and golden in colour when ready.**

3. **Pour in the beaten eggs, along with plenty of salt and pepper, and cook for 4–6 minutes, stirring, until the eggs are just set but not dry.**

4. **Switch off the heat, lay the 4 tortilla wraps out on a chopping board or your clean work surface and divide the mixture evenly between the middle of each one. Sprinkle over the cherry tomatoes and cheese. Roll up each burrito tightly.**

5. **Put the pan back over a low to medium heat and add the remaining oil. Tuck the four burritos into the pan and brown them on all sides. (Keep an eye on them as they can burn, turn them over when each side is golden).**

6. **Cut in half and serve.**

You could replace the sausages here with vegetarian sausages. They won't pop out of their skins in the same way however, so just pan-fry them and then chop them into small pieces, before adding the eggs.

These breakfast burritos freeze really well. Defrost them in the fridge overnight and then, in the morning, wrap them in kitchen paper and microwave until hot through.

ROASTED HONEY-GLAZED PLUMS

20 MINS / SERVE WITH HONEYED YOGHURT

Roasting fruit like this, with a drizzle of citrus and sweetness, turns it into something quite magical. Golden, juicy jewels. Plums are used here but any stone fruit, like apricots, will work well. You can use the same method with apples that have been forgotten in the fridge. I find that adding a handful of chocolate chips (when you sprinkle on the granola) helps entice children to try them.

1. Preheat the oven to 180°C fan/200°C/Gas Mark 6.

2. Carefully cut the stone fruit in half. Do this by holding the fruit carefully and pushing a knife in until you feel the stone, then run the knife all the way around the fruit. Put the knife down, twist each half of the fruit with your hands and they will pop apart. Then scoop the stone out with a spoon.

3. Lay the fruit halves on a baking tray, cut side up.Grate over the zest from the orange and squeeze over the juice. Drizzle over the honey.

4. Bake in the oven for 10–15 minutes or until the fruit is just starting to soften.

5. Remove from the oven and spoon the granola over the top of the sticky fruit, then return to the oven for a further 5 minutes.

SERVES 4

8 plums (or other stone fruit)
1 orange
4 tsp runny honey
75g granola

HONEYED YOGHURT

5 MINS / SERVES 4

A couple of additions to plain Greek yoghurt elevate it to something special here.

400g Greek yoghurt
4 tsp runny honey
2 tsp vanilla extract
1 tsp ground cinnamon

Mix the ingredients together and serve.

If you have any granola left from page 35 this works brilliantly here.

IF YOU'D PREFER TO USE A SLOW COOKER...
These can be cooked on HIGH for 45 minutes. Line the slow cooker with baking paper to prevent them sticking and add the granola at the same time as the other ingredients.

DUTCH BABY

30 MINS / SERVE WITH MANGO SALAD

Yes, this is essentially a giant sweet Yorkshire pudding, light around the edges and slightly pancake-like in the middle. It's such an easy and impressive breakfast or brunch. I opt for a flavourless Dutch Baby as it rises significantly more than when it's made with added sugar or spices. Don't leave out the maple or honey drizzle though as this is what adds all the sweetness.

1. Preheat the oven to 200°C fan/220°C/Gas Mark 7.

2. Put a sauté pan into the oven, with the oil in, to preheat (you can do this while the oven heats up).

3. Mix up the batter by putting the flour into a large bowl and beating in the eggs until smooth. When it has formed a smooth paste with no lumps, gradually add the milk, whisking until smooth.

4. Open the oven door and very carefully pour the batter into the hot pan (do this quickly, keeping the pan almost in the oven if possible – the idea is to keep it as scorching hot as possible!) and bake for 20–25 minutes until risen and golden brown. Don't open the oven door before 20 minutes have passed or it won't rise!

5. Remove from the oven, drizzle over the honey or maple syrup and serve immediately.

SERVES 4

1 tbsp sunflower oil
80g plain flour
4 eggs
160ml semi-skimmed milk
4 tbsp runny honey or maple syrup, to serve

MANGO SALAD

10 MINS / SERVES 4

This fruit salad is as much about the colour as the taste – we eat with our eyes, right?! I like to make double the quantity and keep half in the fridge to eat during the week (it will keep for 2–3 days).

1 ripe mango
150g raspberries
150g blueberries
1 lemon, juiced
1 tsp ground cinnamon

Peel and chop the mango into 1cm cubes. Toss in a bowl with the other ingredients and serve.

MANGO SALAD

YOGHURT BREAKFAST BARK

5 MINS, PLUS FREEZING TIME

I'm not sure this actually counts as a recipe – perhaps more of a kitchen trick. It's a fun breakfast for children to help make (and they love to eat it, so win win). Make it as a Saturday activity and eat it for breakfast on Sunday or during the following week. This is also a good way to use any spare yoghurt that is about to reach its use-by date, as freezing it will prolong its life.

1. **Line a baking tray with baking paper (not greaseproof paper) and smooth over the yoghurt in a thick layer.**

2. **Drizzle over the honey and sprinkle over the granola and fruit.**

3. **Freeze on the tray, uncovered, for at least 3 hours or until you're ready to serve it.**

4. **When you're ready to serve, remove the bark from the baking paper and cut into big chunks.**

SERVES 4

500g full-fat Greek yoghurt
4 tbsp runny honey
150g granola
200g raspberries
200g blueberries

If you want to make a bigger batch and store this in the freezer, cut it into the chunks and return to the freezer in a freezer-proof container or bag (so you can reclaim your baking tray). It will keep in the freezer for up to one month.

You could use lower-fat yoghurt here, but it tends to form ice crystals and be very crunchy when frozen, so please use full fat.

If you have any granola left from the recipes on pages 32–5, this works brilliantly here.

MFAT-FREE MEALS

V

PANEER TIKKA ONE-POT

25 MINS

Paneer is an Indian cheese that holds its shape as it cooks and, when pan-fried is golden and crispy. If you've never tried paneer before, it's worth hunting out (you can find it in most major supermarkets now). The shortcut of using pouches of pre-cooked rice here makes this a really speedy dinner.

1. Heat HALF the oil in a sauté pan over a medium heat. Add the paneer and fry, stirring occasionally, for about 5 minutes until coloured all over.

2. Carefully scoop the paneer from the pan and transfer to a plate lined with kitchen paper.

3. Put the rest of the oil in the pan, add the onion and cauliflower and fry over a medium heat for 5 minutes until just starting to soften.

4. Turn the heat down to low, add the spice paste, chickpeas and water and give everything a good stir. Put the lid on the pan and cook for 5 minutes.

5. Add the rice from the pouches (no need to preheat it) and a good pinch of sea salt. Stir well, using a wooden spoon to break up the rice, then gently add the paneer back in. Cook for a further 5 minutes, stirring occasionally, until the rice is heated.

6. Sprinkle with the fresh mint and serve.

SERVES 4

2 tsp sunflower oil
250g paneer cheese, cut into 2cm cubes
1 red onion, peeled and cut into wedges
500g cauliflower (or 1 whole head), cut into small pieces (about 2cm)
150g tikka masala curry paste (see Notes)
1 x 400g tin chickpeas, drained and rinsed
250ml water
2 x 250g microwave rice pouches
sea salt
10g fresh mint, finely chopped, to serve

When you buy the spice paste (not sauce), check the recommended quantity per person: they are usually 150g for 4 people but occasionally they are sold in a much more concentrated form so you will need less. Double check before scooping it out of the jar, and reduce the measurement if necessary!

MOROCCAN-STYLE AUBERGINE WITH APRICOTS

3 HOURS 15 MINS / **SERVE WITH FETA COUSCOUS PAGE 62**

Even the most ardent aubergine hater out there (and I know, there are many) may be converted by this recipe. If your family are particularly suspicious, cut the offending article even smaller so it almost melts into this rich and flavoursome sauce. This recipe uses the shortcut of ras el hanout spice mix to add heaps of Moroccan flavour. It's available from most large supermarkets now and is definitely worth the space in your spice drawer.

1. **Put all of the ingredients for the slow cook into a slow cooker pot, APART FROM the cornflour and stock, seasoning with salt and pepper.**

2. **Put the cornflour into a small dish and add just enough of the stock to make a smooth paste. Now add that paste back into the measuring jug of stock (we use this method to avoid flour lumps), mix well and add to the rest of the ingredients in the slow cooker.**

3. **Cook on HIGH for 3–4 hours or LOW for 6–8 hours with the lid on until the vegetables are softened and the sauce is thickened.**

4. **Before serving, stir in in the honey and sprinkle the flaked almonds all over.**

SERVES 4

For the Slow Cook
1 tbsp olive oil
1 red onion, peeled and finely chopped
2 aubergines, cut into 2cm cubes
2 x 400g tins chickpeas, drained and rinsed
1 x 400g tin chopped tomatoes
1 tbsp ras el hanout spice mix
2 tsp ground cumin
100g dried apricots, cut into small pieces
2 tbsp cornflour
500ml hot vegetable stock (made with a stock cube is fine)
sea salt and freshly ground black pepper

To Serve
2 tbsp runny honey
30g flaked almonds (toasted, if possible)

You can make this dish vegan by changing the honey for maple syrup (also checking that the stock is vegan).

This recipe is perfect for freezing as a Dump Bag (see page 17). Freeze the 'slow cook' ingredients, minus the cornflour and stock. Add these per the recipe just before cooking.

IF YOU DON'T HAVE A SLOW COOKER...

At step 3 above, cook the 'slow cook' ingredients in a lidded saucepan on the hob (including the cornflour paste), over a low heat, for 30–40 minutes until the vegetables are soft and the sauce is thick. If the sauce is too thick, add an additional 100ml water.

FETA COUSCOUS
p.62

CREAMY VEGETABLE CURRY

5 HOURS 15 MINS

This recipe is infinitely adaptable and a great way to use up whatever vegetables you have in the fridge that need a good home. The only veg I'm not so keen on including is broccoli, as it tends to lose its colour and look a little sad when slow cooked. The mango chutney at the end adds a little sweetness. Serve with warmed naan breads for scooping.

1. Put all of the ingredients into the slow cooker pot with a good pinch of sea salt and give everything a good stir. Put the lid on and cook on HIGH for 5–6 hours or LOW for 8–10 hours, or until the sweet potato is tender.

2. Before serving, stir in the mango chutney and garam masala and sprinkle with the flaked almonds.

SERVES 4

For the Slow Cook
150g korma curry paste (not sauce)
¼ tsp dried chilli flakes
1 onion, peeled and chopped
3 garlic cloves, peeled and crushed
500g sweet potatoes, peeled and cut into 2cm chunks
1 x 400g tin green lentils, drained and rinsed
500g cauliflower (or 1 whole head), cut into bite-sized pieces
1 x 400ml tin reduced-fat coconut milk
sea salt

To Finish
100g mango chutney
2 tsp garam masala
50g flaked almonds (toasted, if possible)

To Serve
naan breads

Check your curry paste label for the suggested serving. It's usually half a jar (about 150g) for 4 people, but it's worth double checking as occasionally they are much stronger and you'll need less.

This recipe is perfect for freezing as a Dump Bag (see page 17). Freeze the 'slow cook' ingredients, minus the coconut milk. Add this as per the recipe just before cooking.

IF YOU DON'T HAVE A SLOW COOKER...
Cook the 'slow cook' ingredients in a saucepan on the hob over a medium heat for 30–40 minutes, adding in the remaining ingredients before serving.

MEAT-FREE MEALS

CRISPY BUTTERNUT SQUASH & FETA PIE

50 MINS / SERVE WITH JEWELLED SALAD PAGE 63

This Moroccan-inspired pie is so simple to make, all in one pan and wrapped up in a filo parcel for the ultimate crunch. It's flavoured with ras el hanout spice mix which is a super shortcut that brings this dish heaps of flavour. Serve this for dinner, or as a vegetarian centrepiece for a special meal.

1. Heat the oil in a sauté pan over a medium heat. Add the onions and garlic and fry for 3–5 minutes until starting to soften. Add the butternut squash and ras el hanout spice mix and cook, uncovered, for 15–20 minutes until the butternut squash is soft and most of the liquid has evaporated.

2. Preheat the oven to 180°C fan/200°C/Gas Mark 6.

3. Spoon the vegetable mixture into a bowl and add the pine nuts and chickpeas then crumble in the feta cheese. Stir until combined but try not to break up all of the lovely cheese chunks.

4. Brush the bottom and sides of the sauté pan you just used with 1 teaspoon of the olive oil for making the pie (no need to clean the pan first). Lay over the sheets of filo pastry so they cover the base and let them flop over the sides of the pan (saving one or two sheets for the top of the pie). This doesn't need to be neat!

5. Spoon in the filling from the bowl and bring the edges of the filo sheets in so that they begin to cover the top of the pie, like a parcel. Drizzle or brush another teaspoon of oil over the pastry. Use the sheets you saved to cover the rest of the top. You can scrunch them up to make them go extra crispy when cooked. Give one last drizzle or brush with another teaspoon of olive oil. Bake in the oven for 20–25 minutes until crisp and golden, then serve.

SERVES 4

For the Filling
2 tsp olive oil
2 red onions, peeled and thinly sliced
3 garlic cloves, peeled and crushed
500g frozen butternut squash cubes (see Notes)
2 tsp ras el hanout spice mix
60g pine nuts (or other nuts)
1 x 400g tin chickpeas, drained and rinsed
100g feta cheese

To Make the Pie
1 tbsp olive oil
270g filo pastry

I use a 500g bag of pre-chopped, frozen butternut squash here as it's such a handy shortcut. If you're using fresh, you'll need to buy a butternut squash heavier than 500g to end up with 500g of flesh left after it's been peeled. You will also need to pan-fry it for longer, probably an additional 15–20 minutes.

JEWELLED SALAD
p.63

SLOW COOKER
MEAT-FREE MONDAY TACOS

6 HOURS / SERVE WITH PINK ONIONS PAGE 62

Tacos are not only simple, tasty and affordable but they are also social and fun to eat as a family. Pile everything on the table and help yourself. It's also a great way to encourage children to try new foods on their own terms as they fill their own tortillas. Often my taco fillings have relied on pan-fried meat, but here I really wanted to come up with a vegetarian alternative that had a deeply savoury, meaty texture. A few tricks (walnuts and Marmite, I'm looking at you) add texture and a depth of flavour.

1. **Open the tins of tomatoes and drain off the liquid using a sieve (we don't want too much of the watery juice).**

2. **Add everything for the slow cook to the slow cooker pot (including the drained tomatoes), season with salt and pepper and give it a good mix. Put a clean tea towel across the top of the slow cooker (this absorbs excess water as condensation) and place the lid on top. Cook on HIGH for 6 hours or LOW for 8–10 hours. The mixture is ready when it's thickened and deep red in colour.**

3. **Serve piled into tortillas (I like to CAREFULLY toast the tortillas over a gas flame to give them some texture, otherwise you can warm them in the oven or microwave) with the avocado slices and feta cheese crumbled on top.**

SERVES 4

For the Slow Cook
2 x 400g tins chopped tomatoes
2 x 400g tins green lentils, drained and rinsed
100g walnuts, finely chopped
2 tbsp tomato purée
1 tbsp ground cumin
1 tbsp sweet smoked paprika
2 tsp garlic granules
1 tbsp Marmite
2 tbsp soft dark brown sugar
sea salt and freshly ground black pepper

To Serve
8 small flour tortillas
1 avocado, halved, peeled, stone removed and sliced
200g feta cheese

If you'd like to make these vegan, omit the feta cheese and serve with a dollop of vegan yoghurt on top instead. Obviously check the ingredients of your tortillas too.

IF YOU DON'T HAVE A SLOW COOKER...
Cook the 'slow cook' ingredients in a large lidded saucepan over a medium heat for 30–40 minutes, stirring every 10 minutes.

PINK ONIONS
p.62

SIDES

FETA COUSCOUS
15 MINS / SERVES 4

V

Couscous is such a handy kitchen standby – it's affordable and there's hardly any cooking required. It is quite forgettable when served plain though, so here we've added a handful of extra flavours to make it something special.

320g couscous
400ml hot vegetable stock
(made with a stock cube is fine)
2 tsp paprika
2 tbsp olive oil
15g fresh mint, finely chopped
100g feta cheese, crumbled
sea salt and freshly ground black pepper

Put the couscous, hot vegetable stock and paprika into a heatproof bowl, mix well and cover with a plate. Leave to stand for 10 minutes.

When the liquid has been absorbed, fluff up the couscous with a fork, add all of the other ingredients and stir well.

PINK ONIONS
20 MINS / SERVES 4

VG

These pink little gems are perfect for serving as an accompaniment to tacos, in sandwiches or over salads. They are super quick to make and add a little extra sparkle to so many dishes. Leave any leftovers in the soaking liquid and store in the fridge for 3–4 days.

1 red onion, peeled and very thinly sliced
(as thinly as you can manage)
100ml white wine vinegar
1 tbsp caster sugar
1 tsp sea salt
100ml boiling water

Put all of the ingredients in a small bowl. Mix well and leave for at least 15 minutes.

Spoon the onion out of the liquid as you serve them.

JEWELLED SALAD
5 MINS / SERVES 4

I was always vaguely surprised by my children's willingness to consume beetroot, until they compared their stained tongues afterwards and it turns out that comedy value in food is often an enticing enough reason to try something new.

80g pomegranate seeds (you can by them in tubs with the fresh, prepared fruit)
250g cooked beetroot, cut into 1cm cubes (the type in the vacuum pack in the supermarket fridge, not in vinegar)
2 apples, cored and cut into 1cm cubes (see Notes)
3 tbsp balsamic vinegar
1 tbsp white wine vinegar
1 tbsp olive oil (extra-virgin if you have it)
5g fresh mint, finely chopped
½ tsp sea salt

Mix all of the ingredients together in a bowl and serve straight away.

I use a Granny Smith apple here as I always have them in the fridge, but also, I like the contrast they bring to the salad as they are a little sour. Feel free to use a sweeter apple or whatever you have available if you prefer, and keep the skin on.

SLOW COOKER
SWEET POTATO & QUINOA CHILLI

3 HOURS 15 MINS

My friend Emma and I often meet in our favourite cafe to work together for the day – working from home alone all week can get lonely. We count down the hours until lunchtime, when we can talk about everything and nothing. Every week we order the same dish as it's SO good, and this is my take on it.

If you've never tried quinoa before (or even if you have) please, give it a chance here. It's a funny looking little grain that you can easily buy in supermarkets now, but it does feel a bit intimidating (and also boring but let's not dwell on that). It works so well here as it soaks up the tasty sauce and gives a texture not entirely dissimilar to meat-based chilli dishes.

1.   **Put everything into a slow cooker and mix well, seasoning with salt and pepper. Cook on HIGH for 3–5 hours or LOW for 6–7 hours, until the sweet potato is just starting to break up and the quinoa is cooked.**

SERVES 4

750g sweet potatoes, peeled and cut into 2cm cubes
1 red onion, peeled and chopped
3 garlic cloves, peeled and crushed
1 x 400g tin black beans, drained and rinsed
1 x 400g tin chopped tomatoes
500g passata
3 tbsp tomato purée
600ml hot vegetable stock
150g quinoa, well rinsed
1 tbsp ground cumin
1 tbsp paprika
1 tbsp ground coriander
1 tbsp mild chilli powder
sea salt and freshly ground black pepper

To Serve
150ml sour cream
100g tortilla chips

I like to serve this as a complete meal in a bowl, with a dollop of sour cream and some tortilla chips for scooping. There are already the carbs within the chilli, so I tend not to bother with rice. Of course, that's up to you though.

When you come to serve the chilli, if you'd like it a little less thick, add an extra 100ml water.

IF YOU DON'T HAVE A SLOW COOKER...
Cook on the hob in a lidded saucepan over a low heat for 25–35 minutes until the vegetables are soft and the sauce is thick. If the sauce becomes too thick, add an extra 100ml water.

NACHO LOADED FRIES

1 HOUR 15 MINS

We love a pile of loaded nachos, but they don't exactly feel like dinner. Here I use homemade chips as a base instead of tortilla chips, and then pile them high with toppings. The end result is all of the favourite flavours of nachos but in a surprisingly nutritious and fuss-free dinner. This version is vegetarian, but of course you could add some cooked chicken or other meats if you fancy. Make sure you cook the chips until they are quite crispy before adding the toppings, so they don't go soggy.

1. Preheat the oven to 200°C fan/220°C/Gas Mark 7.

2. Put the potatoes on a baking tray, drizzle over the oil and sprinkle over the fajita seasoning. Toss so they are totally coated in the oil and the seasoning and bake in the oven for 45 minutes.

3. Flip and cook for another 10–15 minutes until cooked to your preferred level of crunchiness. I like mine very crisp and golden all over!

4. While the chips are cooking, mix the sweetcorn, black beans and salsa together in a bowl.

5. When the chips are ready, remove them from the oven, rearrange them so they are in an even layer on the baking tray, then top them with the salsa mixture, dolloping it over evenly.

6. Sprinkle the mozzarella cheese all over the top and return to the oven for 10 minutes until the cheese is melted and golden.

7. Remove from the oven and serve with the sour cream spooned on top and the spring onions sprinkled over.

SERVES 4

1.25kg white potatoes, such as Maris Piper or King Edward, cut into 1cm-thick chip shapes (no need to peel, unless you want to)
2 tbsp sunflower oil
2 tsp fajita seasoning
1 x 200g tin sweetcorn, drained
1 x 400g tin black beans, drained and rinsed
200g fresh tomato salsa (from the supermarket dips aisle)
200g grated mozzarella cheese

To Serve
150ml sour cream
6 spring onions, finely chopped

SLOW COOKER
SNEAKY VEG MAC & CHEESE

2 HOURS 30 MINS

Dairy-based sauces can be tricky to get right in the slow cooker. They can curdle and end up looking rather depressing when you come to serve them. Here's my solution, which is pain free and has the added benefit of sneaking in a secret portion of hidden vegetable. Don't be tempted to swap in another pasta shape for the macaroni. It's one of the few types of pasta I've found that reliably cooks well in the slow cooker as it doesn't break too easily.

1. **Put the slow cook ingredients into the slow cooker, season with salt and pepper, pop the lid on and cook on HIGH for 2 hours or until the butternut squash is tender.**

2. **Use a hand-held blender to blend the butternut squash along with the liquid it cooked in, to make a smooth sauce. Add the vegetable stock and macaroni. Stir, put the lid on and cook on HIGH for 15–20 minutes until almost cooked.**

3. **Stir in the cheese and mustards, cover and cook for a further 5–10 minutes until the cheese is melted and the pasta is cooked.**

SERVES 4

For the Slow Cook
500g frozen butternut squash cubes
    (see Notes)
300ml water
1 vegetable stock cube (undiluted)
sea salt and freshly ground
    black pepper

To Finish
400ml hot vegetable stock
    (made with a stock cube is fine)
300g dried macaroni pasta
    (uncooked)
250g mature Cheddar cheese,
    grated
1 tsp wholegrain mustard
1 tsp Dijon mustard

I use a 500g bag of pre-chopped, frozen butternut squash here as it's such a handy shortcut. If you're using fresh you'll need to buy a butternut squash that's larger than 500g to end up with 500g of flesh left after it has been peeled. You will also need to cook it for longer, probably an additional 1–2 hours on HIGH.

If you need to cook the butternut squash for longer (because you're out of the house or similar) it's very forgiving BUT the pasta is not, that needs to be cooked for the final cooking time until JUST tender.

IF YOU DON'T HAVE A SLOW COOKER...

Simmer the 'slow cook' ingredients in a saucepan over a medium heat for 15 minutes or until soft enough to purée. Blend, add the stock and dried macaroni (uncooked) and cook for a further 15 minutes until the pasta is almost cooked. Add the cheese and mustards and simmer for another 5 minutes.

HALLOUMI FAJITA-STYLE TRAYBAKE

35 MINS

Baking a fajita filling mixture in the oven is one of my favourite kitchen shortcuts. (Whenever I make the filling in a frying pan, I overfill it – is it just me?!) Anyway, here we've taken those flavours and added rice to make a complete meal.

1. **Preheat the oven to 200°C fan/220°C/Gas Mark 7.**

2. **Put the onions and peppers on a baking tray and drizzle over 2 teaspoons of the oil and 1 tablespoon of the fajita seasoning. Toss well so everything is coated. Bake for 20 minutes until the vegetables are just softened.**

3. **While the vegetables are in the oven, put the halloumi cubes into a small bowl with the remaining teaspoon of oil and tablespoon of fajita seasoning and toss to coat.**

4. **When the vegetables come out of the oven sprinkle the microwave rice pouches onto the tray, no need to preheat it (you may need to use clean hands to break these up as they can be quite clumpy). Give them a good stir so the rice is coated in the vegetable juices.**

5. **Sit the halloumi cubes on top of the rice and return the tray to the oven for 10–15 minutes until the rice is hot and the halloumi is beginning to turn golden.**

6. **Dollop on the sour cream, scatter over the avocado and serve.**

SERVES 4

2 red onions, peeled and cut into 2cm-thick wedges
3 peppers, deseeded and cut into 1cm-thick strips (whatever colour you prefer)
1 tbsp sunflower oil
2 tbsp fajita seasoning (see Notes)
225g halloumi, cut into small cubes
2 x 250g microwave rice pouches (see Notes)

To Serve
150ml sour cream
1 avocado, halved, peeled, stone removed and cut into cubes

I used ready-to-go rice pouches here to truly make this a one-pot recipe, but if you prefer to cook your own, just cook 300g dried long-grain rice according to the packet instructions, drain and use as normal.

The level of spice here should be mild and suitable for children (unless you've bought a particularly hot fajita spice mix!). If you do want some extra heat, use 3 tablespoons seasoning instead of 2 tablespoons.

MEAT-FREE MEALS

PILES OF PASTA

CHICKEN CACCIATORE PASTA

35 MINS

This ingredient list looks longer than my average, but it's all standard fridge and store-cupboard ingredients. These come together (surprisingly quickly) to make a rich, flavourful sauce. Chicken cacciatore is a traditional Italian dish, 'cacciatore' meaning 'hunter style'. This take on the recipe cooks the pasta right in the sauce for a midweek one-pot shortcut.

1. **Heat the olive oil in a sauté pan over a high heat, add the chicken and bacon and cook for 5–7 minutes until turning golden all over.**

2. **Reduce the heat to medium and add the onion, garlic, carrots and chestnut mushrooms and cook for a further 5–7 minutes until the vegetables have started to soften.**

3. **Add the dried pasta, tinned tomatoes, tomato purée, oregano, chilli flakes and stock. Cook, with the lid on, stirring occasionally for 15–20 minutes until the pasta is cooked through and the sauce is thickened.**

4. **To serve, stir in the basil leaves and sprinkle over the Parmesan.**

SERVES 4

1 tsp olive oil
650g skinless, boneless chicken breasts, cut into bite-sized pieces
200g smoked bacon lardons
1 onion, peeled and chopped
3 garlic cloves, peeled and crushed
3 carrots, peeled and cut into small pieces
400g chestnut mushrooms, sliced
250g dried pasta of your choice (uncooked)
1 x 400g tin chopped tomatoes
2 tbsp tomato purée
2 tsp dried oregano
¼ tsp dried chilli flakes
750ml hot vegetable stock (made with a stock cube is fine)
sea salt and freshly ground black pepper

To Serve
20g fresh basil leaves
100g Parmesan cheese, grated

At the end of the cooking time, if your pasta is not cooked and the liquid has been absorbed, just add a splash of water and cook for a little longer.

CREAMY GNOCCHI TRAYBAKE

45 MINS

For me, the holy grail of mid-week dinners is a dish not only made in one pan, but one that also involves very minimal chopping. If (like me) you choose to use those handy ready-prepared bags of frozen butternut squash, that's exactly what this dish offers. Straight to the pan, no chopping with a delicious dinner at the end.

SERVES 4

1kg frozen butternut squash cubes
    (see Notes)
2 tsp olive oil
2 tsp garlic granules
500g long-life ready-made gnocchi
400g cherry tomatoes
165g garlic and herb cream cheese
15g fresh basil
75g Parmesan cheese, grated
sea salt and freshly ground
    black pepper

1. Preheat the oven to 200°C fan/220°C/Gas Mark 7.

2. Put your butternut squash on a baking tray and drizzle over the oil, then sprinkle with the garlic granules and plenty of salt and pepper. Bake in the oven for 20 minutes until starting to soften.

3. Remove from the oven, add the gnocchi and tomatoes and give everything a good stir. Turn the cream cheese out onto the middle of the baking tray (in one lump, no need to spread it around). Put the baking tray back into the oven for 20 minutes.

4. When the butternut squash and the gnocchi are cooked through and starting to colour, remove the tray from the oven, add the basil leaves and stir well to combine the cream cheese with everything.

5. Sprinkle over the Parmesan and add more salt and pepper if needed, then serve.

I use 2 x 500g bags of pre-chopped, frozen butternut squash here as it's such a handy shortcut. If you'd prefer to use fresh butternut squash, you'll need to buy more than 1kg in weight to end up with 1kg of flesh left after it has been peeled and seeds removed.

SPANAKOPITA-STYLE PASTA

20 MINS

This pasta dish is a vague nod to the flavours of the Greek spinach and feta pie. It's cooked in one pan, where the stock and starch from the pasta help to make a silky smooth sauce. I 'shred' the spinach here (so basically just thinly slice it into very thin strips) so that it cooks super quickly and doesn't leave lumpy bits in the sauce, I find this makes it much more user friendly when feeding the children.

1. Put the pasta, vegetable stock and garlic granules in a sauté pan over a medium heat and cook for 5 minutes, stirring occasionally.

2. Add the long-stemmed broccoli pieces, stir well and cook for a further 7–10 minutes with the lid on until the pasta is cooked through and the broccoli is tender.

3. When everything is almost cooked, add the spinach to the pan and stir well – it should wilt almost instantly as you stir.

4. Take the pan off the heat and add the cream cheese, lemon zest, fresh mint and plenty of salt and pepper. Stir the mixture very well until the cream cheese is mixed into the cooking liquid and has formed a smooth sauce.

5. Sprinkle over the crumbled feta cheese and serve.

SERVES 4

300g dried pasta of your choice (uncooked)
900ml hot vegetable stock (made with a stock cube is fine)
2 tsp garlic granules
200g long-stemmed broccoli, cut into bite-sized pieces
240g baby spinach, finely shredded
200g cream cheese
1 lemon, zested and juiced
10g fresh mint, finely chopped
100g feta cheese, crumbled
sea salt and freshly ground black pepper

SAUSAGE GNOCCHI

45 MINS

Using sausage like this, breaking them up and frying until they make a crispy and golden mince, is a handy shortcut for packing lots of flavour into a quick sauce. Here we've added one of those handy store-cupboard standby packs of gnocchi, which cooks straight in the sauce. Top with breadcrumbs for a satisfying crunch.

1. Heat the oil in a sauté pan over a medium-high heat and squeeze the sausages out of their skins into the pan. Use a wooden spoon to break up the sausages. Cook for about 10 minutes, stirring occasionally, until they turn crispy and golden. (They should look something like mince at this point.)

2. Add the onion, garlic and broccoli. Stir over a medium heat for 5 minutes until the broccoli starts to soften, then add the passata, oregano, fennel seeds, dried chilli flakes, honey and plenty of salt and pepper. Cook for a further 10 minutes, stirring occasionally.

3. Preheat the grill to high.

4. To your sauce, add the gnocchi and frozen peas. Cook for a further 5 minutes until the gnocchi is softened.

5. Give everything a good stir, sprinkle the breadcrumbs on top and pop under the grill for 5 minutes until the breadcrumbs are starting to brown.

SERVES 4

1 tsp olive oil
450g pork sausages (or 8 sausages)
1 red onion, peeled and chopped
3 garlic cloves, peeled and crushed
1 head of broccoli (about 300g), cut into very small bite-sized pieces
1kg passata
2 tsp dried oregano
1 tsp fennel seeds
½ tsp dried chilli flakes
2 tsp runny honey
500g long-life ready-made gnocchi
200g frozen peas
75g dried breadcrumbs, such as panko
sea salt and freshly ground black pepper

SLOW COOKER
ONE-PAN LASAGNE

So many of you loved my One-pan Lasagne recipe in my first book that I had to come up with a slow cooker version, and here it is! I've added a pot of ricotta on top here as an instant extra cheesy layer. The pasta cooking time at the end can vary quite a lot – it'll depend on your slow cooker. Use your own judgement and cook until the pasta is the right texture for you.

1. Add all of the slow cook ingredients to the slow cooker pot and season with salt and pepper. Mix everything together, pop the lid on and cook on HIGH for 5 hours or LOW for 7–9 hours until the sauce is thick and rich.

2. Remove the bay leaves and discard. Add the beef stock and give everything and mix to combine with the sauce. Take the dried lasagne sheets and push them into the sauce in the slow cooker, so they are standing up vertically side by side (if you can avoid them touching each other too much as they cook it helps to stop them sticking together). You will need to snap some of them in half (or smaller) to fit them all in. Put the lid back on and cook on HIGH for 15 minutes.

3. Give everything a good stir, moving the softened pasta around so any partially uncooked pieces are now submerged. Now dollop the ricotta cheese all over the surface and sprinkle the mozzarella on top. Put the lid on and cook on HIGH for a further 15–25 minutes, then serve.

OPTIONAL:

If you want the cheese to be crispy and you have a slow cooker pan that is safe to use under the grill (please check!), pop it under a hot grill for 5 minutes until the cheese is golden and bubbling.

SERVES 4

For the Slow Cook
500g beef mince (5% fat)
1 onion, peeled and finely chopped
4 garlic cloves, peeled and crushed
3 celery sticks, finely chopped
3 carrots, peeled and finely chopped
2 x 400g tins chopped tomatoes
75g tomato purée
2 tsp dried oregano
4 tbsp Worcestershire sauce
(or Henderson's Relish)
3 bay leaves
sea salt and freshly ground
black pepper

To Finish
500ml hot beef stock (made with a stock cube is fine)
250g dried lasagne sheets (uncooked)
250g ricotta cheese
100g grated mozzarella cheese

I use grated mozzarella here as it's very easy to keep in the fridge – you can use buffalo mozzarella if you prefer.

IF YOU DON'T HAVE A SLOW COOKER...

You can find the method for a non slow cooker version of this recipe in my first book *What's for Dinner? Fuss-free Family Food in 30 Minutes.*

MEAT FEAST PIZZA PASTA

40 MINS

The pizza on page 172 is surprisingly easy and satisfying to make, but if you can't quite face dusting the kitchen with flour during the week, I give you Pizza Pasta! A sneaky veggie sauce with all the gooey cheese topping that we know and love. You can mix up the toppings and use whatever you like. Leave out the pepperoni and bacon if you'd prefer it to be vegetarian.

1. **Heat the oil in a sauté pan over a high heat. Add the bacon lardons and fry for 5 minutes until crispy.**

2. **Add the onion, garlic, mushrooms and peppers and fry for 5–10 minutes until the vegetables have softened.**

3. **Add the tinned tomatoes, pasta, oregano, vegetable stock and plenty of salt and pepper. Pop the lid on and cook for 13–15 minutes or until the pasta is cooked through and the liquid is absorbed.**

4. **Preheat the grill to medium.**

5. **When the pasta is cooked, stir in the fresh basil. Sprinkle the mozzarella cheese all over the top of the pasta and lay the pepperoni and olives (if using) on top.**

6. **Put under the grill for 5 minutes or until the cheese is melted and golden.**

SERVES 4

1 tbsp olive oil
200g smoked bacon lardons
(or bacon cut into small pieces)
1 onion, peeled and chopped
3 garlic cloves, peeled and crushed
150g chestnut mushrooms, sliced
2 peppers, deseeded and chopped
into 2cm pieces (whichever
colour you prefer)
1 x 400g tin chopped tomatoes
250g dried pasta of your choice
(uncooked)
1 tsp dried oregano
750ml hot vegetable stock
(made with a stock cube is fine)
10g fresh basil, torn into pieces
200g grated mozzarella cheese
50g pepperoni slices
25g sliced olives (optional)
sea salt and freshly ground
black pepper

If you have more time, instead of putting this under the grill you can bake it in the oven at 180°C fan/ 200°C/Gas Mark 6 for 15 minutes. It will become even more crispy and crunchy around the edges.

SLOW COOKER
MUSHROOM ORZOTTO

3 HOURS 40 MINS

This recipe is something like a mushroom risotto but here I've used orzo pasta instead. It's one of the few pastas that I find cook reliably in the slow cooker. Most large supermarkets stock it now, and it's worth hunting out. Oh, and also, please don't be disturbed by the Marmite here! Even if you're a hater, you can't really taste it – it just adds a deeply savoury umami tang.

1. **Put the slow cook ingredients into a slow cooker pot, cover with the lid and cook on HIGH for 3 hours or LOW for 4–5 hours.**

2. **When the mushrooms are soft and the stock has deepened in colour, add the orzo and a good sprinkle of pepper, give everything a good stir, put the lid back on and cook for 30 minutes on HIGH or until the pasta is just tender.**

3. **Switch off the heat and stir in the grated Parmesan cheese and butter until melted. Check for seasoning and add salt or more pepper if needed.**

SERVES 4

For the Slow Cook
400g chestnut mushrooms, thickly sliced
1 onion, peeled and chopped
4 garlic cloves, peeled and crushed
1 tsp dried thyme
700ml water
2 vegetable stock cubes (undiluted)
2 tsp Marmite

To Finish
300g orzo pasta (uncooked)
75g Parmesan cheese, grated
25g butter (salted or unsalted is fine)
sea salt and freshly ground black pepper

If you leave this recipe to stand for a while before serving, or reheat it, it can become a little 'gloopy'. When you're cooking it, be sure to switch off the heat as soon as the pasta is cooked. Also, you can add a splash of water to thin it out a little if needed.

If you're vegetarian and don't eat Parmesan, feel free to substitute in an alternative strongly flavoured hard Italian cheese.

IF YOU DON'T HAVE A SLOW COOKER...

Fry the mushrooms, onion and garlic with 2 teaspoons of olive oil in your sauté pan over a medium heat for 5 minutes or until just softened. Add the thyme, water, stock cubes, Marmite, orzo and some salt and pepper and cook over a medium heat for 10–15 minutes, stirring often, until the pasta is cooked. Add the Parmesan and butter just before serving.

SALMON PRIMAVERA PASTA

20 MINS

The pasta in this recipe cooks right there in the stock, with the starch from the pasta cooking water helping to make a simple sauce when mixed with cream cheese. Primavera pasta is an American creation, rather than an Italian one, and is packed with green vegetables. Here we've added some smoked salmon for protein and flavour, but feel free to leave it out if you'd prefer this to be vegetarian.

1. **Put a sauté pan over a medium heat and add the pasta, vegetable stock and pesto. Pop the lid on and cook for 8 minutes.**

2. **Add the broccoli and peas, give everything a good stir, put the lid back on and cook for a further 5–8 minutes until the broccoli is tender and the pasta is cooked through.**

3. **Remove the pan from the heat. Add the cream cheese, smoked salmon, zest and juice of the lemon and some black pepper (you shouldn't need any salt as there's plenty in the stock and smoked salmon). Stir well until the cream cheese has melted into the sauce, then serve.**

SERVES 4

300g dried pasta of your choice (uncooked)
850ml hot vegetable stock (made with a stock cube is fine)
4 tbsp green pesto
200g long-stemmed broccoli, cut into 4cm pieces
200g frozen peas
100g cream cheese
200g smoked salmon, cut into thin strips
1 lemon, zested and juiced
freshly ground black pepper

This is quite zesty.
You may want to add the juice of just half a lemon first and give it a taste test if your family is not so keen on punchy flavours!

CREAMY BROCCOLI & BEEF TORTELLINI

20 MINS

A pack of dried supermarket tortellini is almost always languishing at the back of my cupboard: on its own it's not terribly inspiring, but here I've bulked it up with broccoli and beef in a vaguely Italian-American-style creamy white sauce (minus the cream!).

1. Heat the oil in a sauté pan over a high heat. Add the mince and fry for 5 minutes, breaking it up with a wooden spoon as it cooks.

2. When the meat has started to brown, add the garlic and the broccoli pieces. Fry for 3 minutes until they have just started to colour.

3. Reduce the heat to medium and sprinkle over the flour, stir for a couple of minutes until everything is coated (doing this first before adding the liquid avoids any lumps), then pour in the milk and mix well.

4. Sprinkle in the chilli flakes and oregano, then add plenty of salt and pepper and the tortellini. Give everything a good stir, put the lid on and cook for 5–8 minutes (stirring occasionally) until the pasta is cooked through and the sauce is thickened. (If the sauce is too thick and the pasta isn't cooked yet, just add a splash more milk.)

5. Serve sprinkled with the Parmesan cheese.

SERVES 4

2 tbsp olive oil
500g beef mince
  (5% or 10% fat is fine)
3 garlic cloves, peeled and crushed
1 head of broccoli (about 300g),
  cut into a similar size to the
  tortellini pieces
50g plain flour
800ml milk (semi-skimmed
  or full-fat)
pinch of dried chilli flakes
1 tsp dried oregano
500g dried tortellini
  (usually 2 x 250g packs)
sea salt and freshly ground
  black pepper

To Serve
50g Parmesan cheese, grated

I use dried tortellini here, which can normally be found where the dried pasta is on the supermarket shelves (rather than in the fridge). You can use fresh, from the fridge section, if you prefer, but you may need to reduce the cooking time slightly.

SLOW COOKER
ITALIAN-STYLE BRAISED BEEF WITH ORZO

6 HOURS SERVE WITH GREMOLATA

This recipe is a rich, tomato-based beef stew, with pasta cooked right there in the sauce. The orzo soaks up the flavours and is similar in texture to a risotto, punctuated with tasty chunks of meat and vegetables. Keep an eye on the orzo as it cooks – it sometimes needs a splash more water added for it to cook all the way through.

1. **Put the slow cook ingredients into a slow cooker pot, season with salt and pepper, give everything a good stir and put the lid on. Cook on HIGH for 5–7 hours or LOW for 8–10 hours, until the beef is tender.**

2. **When the beef is soft, add the orzo, beef stock and cherry tomatoes, put the lid back on and cook for 45 minutes on HIGH.**

3. **Before serving, turn off the heat and stir in the butter and grated Parmesan.**

SERVES 4

For the Slow Cook
400g diced beef (see Notes)
1 onion, peeled and chopped
3 garlic cloves, peeled and chopped
250g chestnut mushrooms, sliced
1 x 400g tin chopped tomatoes
500g passata
2 tbsp balsamic vinegar
1 tbsp dried oregano
sea salt and freshly ground
    black pepper

To Finish
200g orzo (uncooked)
350ml hot beef stock (made with
    a stock cube is fine)
200g cherry tomatoes
50g salted butter
75g Parmesan cheese, grated

GREMOLATA

10 MINS / SERVES 4

Gremolata sounds super fancy but bear with me. It is a nifty 3-ingredient Italian condiment that takes so many dishes from an 8/10 to a 10/10. Serve it on top of any tomato-based pasta dish, over cooked veggies or on top of beef stew.

30g fresh parsley, very finely chopped
1 lemon, zested
1 garlic clove, peeled and crushed

**Mix the ingredients together well
in a bowl and serve as a condiment.**

This recipe would be perfect for freezing as a Dump Bag (see page 17). Freeze just the 'slow cook' ingredients.

'Diced beef/cubed beef' is any kind of beef suitable for slow cooking/stewing, as sold in supermarkets and butchers. I find that they vary greatly in size, shape and tenderness so you may need to adjust the cooking time until the meat is tender.

PILES OF PASTA

IF YOU DON'T HAVE A SLOW COOKER...

Cook the 'slow cook' ingredients in the oven, in a lidded casserole dish, for 2½ hours at 160°C fan/ 180°C/Gas Mark 4. When the beef is tender, add the orzo, stock and cherry tomatoes, cover and return to the oven for 20–25 minutes until the orzo is cooked. Finish as per recipe.

CAPRESE PASTA

25 MINS

This one-pan pasta dish is in the style of the classic Italian Caprese salad, with plenty of tomatoes and buffalo mozzarella. I've used pesto rather than fresh basil as a good store-cupboard shortcut, but feel free to add some fresh basil if you happen to have any that needs using up. The cheese should just begin to melt as you serve the finished dish – simply heaven.

1. Heat the oil in a sauté pan over a medium heat. Add the onion and garlic and cook for 5 minutes until just starting to soften.

2. Add the dried pasta, tinned tomatoes, vegetable stock, tomato purée, pesto, spinach and some salt and pepper. Give everything a good mix, put the lid on and cook for 5 minutes.

3. Add the cherry tomatoes to the pasta, cover and cook for a further 10 minutes or until the pasta is cooked and most of the liquid has been absorbed.

4. When the pasta is cooked, check for seasoning, adding more salt and pepper if needed. Remove from the heat and stir in the balsamic vinegar. Rip the mozzarella cheese into big chunks and stir through the pasta just before serving.

SERVES 4

2 tsp olive oil
1 onion, peeled and chopped
4 garlic cloves, peeled and crushed
300g dried pasta of your choice (uncooked)
1 x 400g tin chopped tomatoes
750ml hot vegetable stock (made with a stock cube is fine)
4 tbsp tomato purée
3 tbsp green pesto
200g frozen spinach (see Notes)
300g cherry tomatoes
2 tbsp balsamic vinegar
125g buffalo mozzarella
sea salt and freshly ground black pepper

I use frozen spinach here as it's so easy to keep in stock. If you prefer to use fresh, don't add it with the pasta, just add it 1 minute before the end of the cooking time so it wilts down.

BAKES & BREADS

CUMIN-CRUSTED LAMB BAKE

50 MINS / SERVE WITH COOLING CUCUMBER SALAD PAGE 112

This spiced lamb traybake uses a simple spice paste to add heaps of flavour to not only the meat, but also all of the vegetables. Cauliflower, which I find is often overlooked in its pale, boiled state, is actually the star of the show when roasted here.

1. Preheat the oven to 200°C fan/220°C/Gas Mark 7.

2. In a small bowl, mix together the spice paste ingredients until it forms a runny paste.

3. Put the potatoes and cauliflower into a large bowl and add HALF the spice paste. Use a spoon or clean hands to coat the vegetables. Spread out on a baking tray and pop into the oven for 25 minutes. (Don't wash the bowl up!)

4. While the potatoes and cauliflower are cooking, add the lamb steaks to the large bowl, add the remaining spice paste and coat them well. Cover and set aside.

5. When the timer is up, remove the baking tray from the oven and give everything a good mix. Nestle the coated lamb steaks in among the vegetables and return to the oven for 15 minutes.

6. Remove the tray from the oven, sprinkle over the spinach and spring onions and stir to combine.

7. Return to the oven for 5 minutes or until the lamb is cooked through and the spinach is wilted.

8. Before serving, squeeze over the juice from the limes or serve with lime halves for everyone to squeeze themselves.

SERVES 4

1kg white potatoes, such as Maris Piper or King Edward, cut into 3cm cubes (no need to peel)
500g cauliflower (or 1 whole head), cut into bite-sized chunks
4 lamb steaks (about 600g in total)
100g baby spinach leaves, cut into thin strips
8 spring onions, finely chopped
sea salt and freshly ground black pepper

For the Spice Paste
1 tbsp ground cumin
1 tbsp ground coriander
1 tbsp garam masala
1 tbsp sunflower oil

To Serve
2 limes, halved

COOLING CUCUMBER SALAD
p.112

PESTO ROAST PORK

50 MINS

When you're in the mood for a roast, but don't want all of the faff of a roast, try this one-pan method. But sssshhh, don't tell anyone how easy it is as it looks far more impressive than the effort involved. If you'd like your prosciutto extra crispy, pop the meat under the grill for a couple of minutes before serving.

4 baking potatoes (700–900g in total), cut into 3cm cubes (no need to peel)
2 tbsp olive oil
2 tsp garlic granules
1 pork fillet, also known as tenderloin (about 500g)
2 tbsp green pesto
90g prosciutto slices
200g green beans, trimmed
sea salt and freshly ground black pepper

1. Preheat the oven to 180°C fan/200°C/Gas Mark 6.

2. Put the cubed potatoes on a baking tray and drizzle with 1 tablespoon of the oil, then season with the garlic granules and plenty of salt and pepper. Use a spoon or clean hands to give everything a good mix so that the potatoes are coated. Bake in the oven for 15 minutes.

3. While the potatoes are starting to cook, take your pork fillet, smother it with the pesto and wrap it in the prosciutto slices. (If you want this to look neat, lay the prosciutto slices on a plate or chopping board – overlapping them slightly – then sit the pork on top, cover it with the pesto and then tightly roll it up.)

4. When the potatoes have been cooking for 15 minutes, remove the tray from the oven, give them a good shuffle around and flip them over, move them to one side of the tray and put the pork onto the baking tray too. Return to the oven for 20 minutes.

5. Finally, add the beans to the tray and drizzle with the remaining tablespoon of oil. Return to the oven for a further 10–15 minutes, until the beans are just softened, the prosciutto is starting to colour and the pork is cooked through.

6. Slice the meat and serve with the vegetables.

SLOW COOKER
STICKY GINGER PULLED HAM

6 HOURS 20 MINS / SERVE WITH PINEAPPLE CRUNCH SALAD PAGE 113

Cooking a gammon joint in any tasty liquid keeps it beautifully tender. Here I use ginger ale for rich, flavoursome sweetness. The addition of some apricot jam at the end of the cooking time coats the meat in an instant sticky sauce. Serve this piled into baguettes or rolls, or use as a sandwich filling.

1. Unwrap the gammon joint (remove all of the packaging, including an inner paper wrapper if your meat has one). Put it into a slow cooker and pour over the ginger ale. Put the lid on the slow cooker and cook on HIGH for 6–8 hours or LOW for 10–12 hours, until the meat is falling apart when you push a fork into it.

2. Drain the meat (discard the cooking liquid) and shred it in the slow-cooker pot using two forks. Spoon in the apricot jam, ground ginger and garlic granules and mix them through the shredded meat. Cover with the lid and cook for a further 15 minutes on LOW until the meat is sticky.

3. Serve piled into the bread.

SERVES 4

For the Slow Cook
750g smoked gammon joint
1 litre ginger ale

To Finish
150g apricot jam
2 tsp ground ginger
1 tsp garlic granules

To Serve
4 bread rolls or baguettes, to serve

This is a great recipe to double up so you have leftovers for sandwiches during the week. Use two pieces of gammon, each 750g, or one larger piece. Double all of the other ingredients apart from the ginger ale. The cooking time will remain the same for two small pieces, but if you're using one larger piece it might take longer: cook it until the meat is falling apart.

IF YOU DON'T HAVE A SLOW COOKER...
Put the gammon and ginger ale into a large saucepan, put the lid on and cook over a low heat for 45–60 minutes, or until the meat is very soft. Continue as above, but warm through for 5 minutes back in the saucepan.

PINEAPPLE
CRUNCH SALAD

p.113

ROASTED OREGANO & LEMON CHICKEN WRAPS

1 HOUR 10 MINS

This is a nod to Greek gyros, but baked in the oven, on one tray, for a simple dinner. If you prefer your chicken to be a little blackened at the edges, feel free to pop it under a very hot grill for a few minutes before slicing, or if the sun is shining, cook the meat on the barbecue instead. This list of ingredients may seem slightly longer than my average, but most of it is for the end assembly job so please don't be put off – the recipe itself is super simple.

1. Preheat the oven to 200°C fan/220°C/Gas Mark 7.

2. In a small bowl, mix the paste ingredients together.

3. Put the potatoes into a larger bowl and add HALF the spice paste. Toss using a spoon or clean hands so that the potatoes are totally coated. Spread them out on a baking tray and cook in the oven for 30 minutes. (Don't wash the bowl up!)

4. While the potatoes are cooking, add the chicken breasts to the bowl that you used to coat the potatoes and add the remaining spice paste. Use a spoon or clean hands to coat the chicken fully.

5. After the timer for the chips goes off, shuffle them and flip them over, move them slightly to one side and add the chicken breasts to the tray. Return to the oven for 25 minutes, or until the chips are golden and the chicken is cooked through (use a meat thermometer if you have one to check).

6. While the chicken and chips finish cooking, prepare the salad vegetables and warm the flatbreads (wrap the breads in foil and add to the oven for the last 10 minutes of cooking time).

7. Transfer the cooked chicken to a chopping board and slice it thinly.

8. Spread the warmed flatbreads with the Greek yoghurt, pile in the chicken, chips and salad. Squeeze a little lemon juice over the filling of each one, roll up and serve.

SERVES 4

750g white potatoes, such as Maris Piper or King Edward, cut into 1cm-thick sticks (no need to peel)
4 skinless, boneless chicken breasts (about 650g in total)

For the Spice Paste
3 tbsp olive oil
1 tbsp sweet smoked paprika
4 tsp garlic granules
2 tsp dried thyme
2 tsp dried oregano
sea salt and freshly ground black pepper

To Serve
1 cucumber, thinly sliced
½ red onion, peeled and thinly sliced
2 salad tomatoes, thinly sliced
4 large flatbreads (wraps or naan breads are fine too)
125g Greek yoghurt
1 lemon, juice only

SAUSAGE PUFF PIE

1 HOUR 10 MINS

For me, making someone a pie is an act of love. This one has a complete meal hiding beneath the pastry, making it even easier to deliver a dose of the ultimate comfort food on a weeknight. I think a herby sausage like a Cumberland works particularly well here to give extra flavour.

1. **Heat the oil in a sauté pan over a high heat, add the sausages and brown them all over: this should take 5–10 minutes.**

2. **Cut each sausage into 3 pieces (I use scissors to do this while they're still the pan), then add the onions, carrots and new potatoes. Fry for another 5–10 minutes until the vegetables have started to soften.**

3. **Turn the heat down to medium, add the flour and stir so that everything is well coated. Add the dried sage and 750ml of the beef stock (keep the rest of the stock to one side). Stir everything well, add the bay leaves and put the lid on the pan. Simmer for 20–25 minutes, checking as it cooks and adding the rest of the stock if it's starting to thicken too much. (I do normally need the full litre, but it will depend on your pan, the heat of your hob and your gravy thickness preferences!)**

4. **Preheat the oven to 200°C fan/220°C/Gas Mark 7.**

5. **When the gravy is thick and the potatoes and carrots are cooked through, remove the pan from the heat. Remove and discard the bay leaves. Add the peas and redcurrant jelly and stir well.**

6. **Roll out the pastry onto the top of the 'pie' and tuck it in around the edges of the sauté pan (you may need to cut one end off to adjust the size and make a square). Be careful, you'll need to work very quickly here as the dish will be hot and will melt the pastry!**

7. **Brush with the beaten egg and bake for 25 minutes until the pastry is golden.**

SERVES 4

2 tsp sunflower oil
450g pork sausages (or 8 sausages)
2 onions, peeled and thinly sliced
4 carrots, peeled and cut into 2cm chunks
500g new potatoes, quartered into roughly 3cm cubes
40g plain flour
1 tbsp dried sage
1 litre hot beef stock (made with a stock cube is fine)
2 bay leaves
200g frozen peas
2 tbsp redcurrant jelly
320g ready-rolled puff pastry
1 egg, beaten
sea salt and freshly ground black pepper

This is a good recipe to prepare in advance. Make up to step 4, then cover and chill for up to 3 days (or freeze). When you're ready to eat, add the pastry and bake as normal (defrosting the filling first, if necessary).

You can easily replace the pork sausages with vegetarian sausages and use vegetable stock.

CHICKEN & FETA TRAYBAKE

1 HOUR 10 MINS

I like to use chicken thighs here as they are affordable and very tender when baked. I opt for skinless and boneless as they are easier to eat, but if you prefer them with bone in, feel free (they may need a slightly longer cooking time). Be sure to cut the courgettes fairly small here or they won't cook in time (I also like to do this to hide them from my courgette-hating children). The salty feta crumble that tops this dish, contrasting with the fresh vegetables, is the stuff my cheesy dreams are made of.

1. Preheat the oven to 180°C fan/200°C/Gas Mark 6.

2. Put the olive oil, garlic granules, oregano, paprika and the zest of the lemon (save the rest of the lemon for later) into a large bowl and mix well.

3. Add the chicken thighs, potatoes and red onions and toss everything together until well coated.

4. Spread out on a baking tray and cook for 45 minutes until everything is starting to colour and the potatoes are almost cooked.

5. Add the courgettes and tomatoes and give everything a good stir so they are coated in the cooking oils. Crumble the feta over the top.

6. Return to the oven for 15 minutes until everything is cooked through and coloured.

7. Squeeze over the juice from the lemon before serving.

SERVES 4

2 tbsp olive oil
2 tsp garlic granules
1 tbsp dried oregano
1 tbsp paprika
1 lemon
900g skinless, boneless chicken thighs
750g white potatoes, such as Maris Piper or King Edward, cut into 3cm chunks (no need to peel)
2 red onions, peeled and quartered (or 1 onion if they are very large)
2 courgettes, cut into 2cm chunks
200g cherry tomatoes
100g feta cheese
sea salt and freshly ground black pepper

STICKY PORK MEATBALLS

45 MINS

A dish has to be quite special for me to bother fiddling with rolling meatballs. Thankfully the rest of this recipe is so simple, it's worth that small effort at the start. This is my top tip; when you've mixed everything for the meatballs together, tip the mixture out onto a chopping board. Cut the mixture in half, then each half in half again, and repeat until you have 16 evenly-sized pieces. Then roll into balls. EASY!

1. Preheat the oven to 180°C fan/200°C/Gas Mark 6.

2. Make the meatballs by mixing the pork mince, garlic granules, Chinese 5-spice and the bottom half of the bunch of spring onions, thinly sliced (save the green part – the top half – to garnish at the end), in a bowl. Use clean hands to mix everything together and form 16 meatballs. (See tip above about shaping the meatballs!)

3. Put the meatballs on a baking tray and pop into the oven for 10 minutes.

4. Remove the tray from the oven, flip the meatballs over and shuffle them to one end of the tray. Add the broccoli florets to the other side of the tray, drizzle with the oil and return to the oven for a further 10 minutes.

5. While this is in the oven, mix the sauce ingredients in a small jug.

6. Remove the tray from the oven and add the sugar snap peas and the noodles (use your fingers to separate them – they'll often come out of the packet in a clump). Drizzle over the sauce, give everything a good stir and return to the oven for 10 minutes.

7. Check that the meatballs are cooked through, and the vegetables are softened, mix everything well and serve with the green parts of the spring onions, sliced and sprinkled on top.

SERVES 4

1 head of broccoli (about 300g), cut into small florets
2 tsp sunflower oil
150g sugar snap peas
300g straight-to-wok noodles (or dried noodles, see Notes below)

For the Meatballs
500g pork mince (about 10% fat)
2 tsp garlic granules
2 tsp Chinese 5-spice
8 spring onions, thinly sliced

For the Sauce
4 tbsp dark soy sauce (I use reduced salt)
2 tbsp runny honey
2 tbsp oyster sauce
2 tbsp sweet chilli sauce

I use straight-to-wok noodles here as a shortcut, but you can use 250g dried medium egg noodles if you prefer; you just need to soak them in just-boiled water after putting the meatballs in the oven. They should be soft and ready to eat by the time they need to be added to the oven (drain them first, obviously!).

BAKES & BREADS

SIDES

COOLING CUCUMBER SALAD
10 MINS / SERVES 4

This simple little side salad pairs well with any dish that has some spice: both the cucumber and yoghurt are fresh and cooling.

1 cucumber, cut into 1cm pieces
200g natural yoghurt
10g fresh mint, finely chopped
½ tsp garlic granules
1 tsp ground cumin
½ tsp sea salt

Mix all of the ingredients together in a bowl and serve immediately.

Greek yoghurt would also work well here. You may want to add a splash of water to get it to the consistency you prefer.

RED SLAW
10 MINS / SERVES 4

This simple slaw is tasty base for the rich taco meat on page 118 but works equally well as a side dish or with some chicken or ham for a light lunch.

½ red cabbage, finely shredded
2 carrots, peeled and grated
1 onion, peeled and thinly sliced

For the Dressing
4 tbsp sunflower oil
2 tbsp runny honey
1 tsp ground cumin
½ tsp garlic granules
½ tsp sea salt

Mix the dressing ingredients in a large bowl until well combined. Add the vegetables and toss to fully coat.

PINEAPPLE CRUNCH SALAD
10 MINS / SERVES 4

I buy a pre-chopped pack of fresh pineapple here and just cut it up a little more, but feel free to prepare your own.

300g fresh pineapple chunks,
cut into 1cm cubes
½ white cabbage, finely shredded
1 red pepper, deseeded and cut
into very thin strips
½ red onion, peeled and thinly sliced
1 lime, zested and juiced
2 tbsp sweet chilli sauce

Mix all of the ingredients together in a bowl and serve immediately.

★

At a pinch you could use tinned pineapple (in juice), drained.

BEEF & MUSHROOM POT PIE

This pie is packed with potatoes and vegetables, making it a complete meal in one dish. The mushrooms add a depth of rich, savoury flavour to the gravy. Ever the mushroom haters, my children will leave every mushroom on the side of the plate, but still I try. Maybe one day?!

1. Preheat the oven to 160°C fan/180°C/Gas Mark 4.

2. Heat the oil in a sauté pan over a high heat, add the diced beef and fry for about 5 minutes until browned all over.

3. Add the onion, carrots and mushrooms and cook for 5 minutes until the onion has started to soften. Reduce the heat to medium, sprinkle over the flour and cook for 5 minutes, stirring until everything is totally coated.

4. Add the potatoes, stock, thyme, tomato purée, Worcestershire sauce and plenty of salt and pepper. Stir everything until combined.

5. Put the lid on the pan and cook in the oven for 2–3 hours or until the beef is very tender. (Give it a stir about halfway through if possible.)

6. Remove the pan from the oven and when you're ready to bake the pie, turn the oven temperature up to 200°C fan/220°C/Gas Mark 7.

7. Unroll your pastry and top the pie with it. Be careful as obviously the pan will be hot – you'll need to work quickly as the heat of the pan will melt the pastry. Just tuck in any excess pastry around the pie filling. Make a small cut or two in the middle. Brush the pastry with the beaten egg and bake for 30 minutes until golden and crisp.

SERVES 4

1 tbsp sunflower oil
500g diced beef
1 onion, peeled and chopped
3 carrots, peeled and cut into 2cm chunks
400g chestnut mushrooms, halved
50g plain flour
500g white potatoes, such as Maris Piper or King Edward, peeled and cut into 3cm cubes
900ml hot beef stock (made with a stock cube is fine)
2 tsp dried thyme
3 tbsp tomato purée
3 tbsp Worcestershire sauce (or Henderson's Relish)
320g ready-rolled shortcrust pastry
1 egg, beaten
sea salt and freshly ground black pepper

You could make the pie filling mixture in advance, then add the pastry and bake at a later time. Keep in the fridge for up to 3 days before adding the pastry and baking. The filling mixture also freezes really well.

CAJUN-STYLE PRAWN TRAYBAKE

40 MINS

Cajun food uses what's known as 'the holy trinity' base of onion, celery and green pepper to help give that distinctive flavour. Here, these ingredients are roasted, and I use a Cajun seasoning (available in most supermarkets) and pre-cooked rice pouches for a shortcut super tasty meal. The level of Cajun spicing here should be mild and suitable for children (unless you've bought a particularly fiery spice mix!), but if you're concerned about any heat, start with just 2 teaspoons of seasoning.

1. Preheat the oven to 200°C fan/220°C/Gas Mark 7.

2. Put the onion, celery and peppers on a baking tray, drizzle with 1 teaspoon of the sunflower oil and season with plenty of salt and pepper. Bake for 15 minutes.

3. While the vegetables are cooking, put the prawns onto a plate and pat them with kitchen paper to dry them. Sprinkle over HALF of the Cajun seasoning to coat them.

4. Remove the tray from the oven and add the rice (no need to preheat it). The rice from these pouches can be quite 'clumpy' so you may need to crumble it onto the tray using clean fingers.

5. Add the sweetcorn to the tray, drizzle over the rest of the oil and sprinkle over the remaining seasoning. Stir well so everything is coated.

6. Sit the coated prawns on top of the rice and return to the oven for 15 minutes.

7. Check that the prawns are completely pink (a sign they are cooked through) and sprinkle with the spring onions before serving.

SERVES 4

1 onion, peeled and finely chopped
4 celery sticks, finely chopped
3 green peppers, deseeded and cut into 1cm pieces
2 tsp sunflower oil
360g raw peeled king prawns (see Notes)
4 tsp Cajun seasoning
2 x 250g microwave rice pouches (see Notes)
1 x 325g tin sweetcorn, drained
sea salt and freshly ground black pepper
6 spring onions, finely chopped, to serve

I used ready-to-go rice pouches here to truly make this a one-pot recipe, but if you prefer to cook your own, just boil 300g dried long-grain rice as per the packet instructions, drain and use as normal.

If you can't find raw king prawns, just use cooked and heat them through. The cooking time won't vary too much but try not to overcook them. You can also buy them frozen and defrost before cooking, if you prefer.

BAKES & BREADS

SLOW COOKER
BRAISED BEEF TACOS

4 HOURS 15 MINS / SERVE WITH RED SLAW PAGE 112

Beef brisket is always best cooked very gently, for a long time, so of course, the slow cooker lends itself perfectly to this. Is the pan-frying beforehand vital? Maybe not. Is it worth 10 minutes of your time to add a LOT of extra flavour? Yes, I think it is. And you know, I will take the lazy cooking route normally, so this must tell you how good these are! The cooked meat freezes well and is also perfect in sandwiches or over rice.

1. Mix all the spices together with the oil, oregano and garlic granules in a large bowl to form a paste.

2. Remove the packaging and any string from the beef, if it has it. (When you remove the string from the meat, it may unravel, this is fine.) Add the beef to the bowl of spice paste and roll it around so all sides are covered. (It is easiest to do this using clean hands).

3. Put the slow cooker pot (if it's suitable for hob use) over a high heat on the hob and, when hot, add the beef. Brown the beef on one side for about 5 minutes before turning it over, then repeat until all surfaces are a deep brown colour. If the slow cooker pot is not suitable for hob use, you'll need to use a sauté pan here.

4. Remove the pot from the heat and put into the slow cooker. Add the tinned tomatoes, tomato purée and stock cubes, crumbling the cubes into the pot. Give everything a good stir, pop the lid on and cook on HIGH for 4–6 hours or LOW for 6–8 hours.

5. When the meat is cooked and easy to pull apart, shred it in the pot using two forks (if it doesn't fall apart easily, it's not cooked yet).

6. Serve the beef piled into the tortillas, topped with a sprinkle of grated cheese.

SERVES 4

1kg beef brisket
1 x 400g tin chopped tomatoes
2 tbsp tomato purée
2 x beef stock cubes (undiluted)
sea salt and freshly ground
    black pepper

For the Spice Paste
1 tbsp ground cumin
1 tbsp sweet smoked paprika
2 tsp mild chilli powder
3 tbsp sunflower oil
2 tsp dried oregano
2 tsp garlic granules

To Serve
8 small tortillas
80g cheese, grated (I used Cheddar, but whichever cheese you fancy is fine)

A lot of fat can come off the brisket as it fries. You can drain this off, before shredding the beef. Gently tip or spoon the layer of fat off the top of the sauce, then add the meat back to the sauce, shred and stir.

IF YOU DON'T HAVE A SLOW COOKER...
After browning the brisket as above, cook it in the oven at 160°C fan/180°C/Gas Mark 4 in a lidded casserole dish for 2½–3½ hours, with an additional 100ml water. Check while cooking to ensure that it's not drying out and add a little more water if needed.

RED SLAW →
p.112

FISHERMAN'S BAKE

1 HOUR 5 MINS

This one-pan meal resembles a fish pie, but doesn't require three pans and a potato masher. It also includes roasted new potatoes nestling in the creamy sauce, which never fail to be a joy. You can use frozen fish pie mix here if you prefer (which is handy to keep on standby). Defrost it before use and cook as normal.

1. Preheat the oven to 180°C fan/200°C/Gas Mark 6.

2. Put the oil and new potatoes in a sauté pan with a good sprinkle of salt and pepper and roast for 40 minutes (uncovered) until starting to turn golden all over.

3. While the potatoes are in the oven, make the sauce. Put the cornflour in a medium bowl and add enough of the milk to make a smooth paste. Add the crème fraîche and whisk until smooth, then add the lemon zest and juice, parsley, the remaining milk and plenty of salt and pepper. Whisk again until smooth.

4. Remove the pan of potatoes from the oven and add the fish (and prawns, if using), peas and the sauce and give everything a good stir. Sprinkle over the breadcrumbs, return the pan to the oven and bake for 20–25 minutes until the breadcrumbs are golden and the fish is cooked.

SERVES 4

1 tbsp olive oil
1kg new potatoes, halved
    or quartered into roughly
    3cm pieces
50g cornflour
500ml milk (semi-skimmed
    or full-fat)
300ml crème fraîche
2 lemons, zested and juiced
4 tsp dried parsley
320g fish pie mix (fresh, or frozen
    and defrosted)
150g raw peeled prawns (see Notes)
200g frozen peas
75g dried breadcrumbs,
    such as panko
sea salt and freshly ground
    black pepper

Fish can be very expensive, so omit
the prawns here if you'd like to
make it more affordable. Fresh or
frozen and defrosted prawns are
fine here.

CHICKEN TIKKA-STYLE TRAYBAKE

55 MINS

This tasty traybake uses the shortcuts of rice pouches and a jar of curry paste, to make one of my easiest, go-to dinners. When you fancy a takeaway, try this instead, it will be ready in the same time, save money and includes two portions of veg. What's not to love?!

1. Preheat the oven to 200°C fan/220°C/Gas Mark 7.

2. Cut the chicken into bite-sized pieces and put onto the baking tray. (I cut each fillet into 3 with scissors straight onto the tray). Add HALF the curry paste and mix to coat the chicken. Spread the chicken out evenly and bake for 25 minutes.

3. Put the peppers, onion and tomatoes in a large bowl, along with the remaining curry paste and mix with a spoon until everything is totally coated.

4. Remove the tray of chicken from the oven and add the coated vegetables. Return to the oven for 15 minutes.

5. Open the pouches of microwave rice and crumble them over the traybake (no need to preheat the rice) – you will probably need to use clean hands to break them up. Add a sprinkle of sea salt, mix well with everything else on the tray and pop back into the oven for 5 more minutes.

6. While this is cooking, mix the mint sauce ingredients in a bowl.

7. Remove from the oven, check that the chicken is cooked through, give everything a good mix and serve with the mint sauce.

SERVES 4

900g skinless, boneless chicken thighs
150g tikka masala curry paste (not sauce)
3 peppers, deseeded and cut into large wedges (whichever colour you prefer)
1 red onion, peeled and cut into wedges
6 salad tomatoes (about 360g total), quartered
2 x 250g microwave rice pouches (see Notes)
sea salt

For the Mint Sauce
200g Greek yoghurt
4 tsp mint sauce (the vinegary type, not jelly)
2 tbsp water
½ tsp sea salt

I used ready-to-go rice pouches here to truly make this a one-pot recipe, but if you prefer to cook your own, just cook 300g dried long-grain rice as per the packet instructions, drain and use as normal.

COMFORT FOOD

SLOW COOKER
CHICKEN TACO SOUP

3 HOURS 25 MINS

This soup has all our favourite taco flavours, but in a tasty broth. It also happens to look particularly gorgeous when piled into a bowl with the toppings. Tortilla chips to scoop are not optional!

SERVES 4

1. **Put all of the slow cook ingredients into the slow cooker pot, season with salt and pepper, put the lid on and cook on HIGH for 3–4 hours or LOW for 4–5 hours.**

2. **When the chicken is cooked through, transfer the two chicken breasts to a plate and shred them into small pieces using two forks.**

3. **Add the shredded chicken back to the slow cooker, along with the sweetcorn. Put the lid on and cook for 15 minutes on HIGH to heat the sweetcorn.**

4. **Squeeze the lime juice into the soup and serve topped with sour cream, grated cheese and the tortilla chips.**

For the Slow Cook
300g skinless, boneless chicken breasts (or a pack of 2)
1 onion, peeled and finely chopped
500g passata
1 x 400g tin chopped tomatoes
1 x 400g tin black beans, drained and rinsed
500ml hot chicken stock (made with a stock cube is fine)
1 tbsp garlic granules
1 tbsp ground cumin
1 tsp dried oregano
1 tsp mild chilli powder
sea salt and freshly ground black pepper

To Finish
1 x 325g tin sweetcorn, drained
1 lime, juiced
75ml sour cream (or yoghurt)
50g Cheddar cheese, grated
100g tortilla chips

You can make this soup vegetarian by replacing the chicken breasts with an additional tin of beans of your choice and swapping the chicken stock for vegetable stock.

IF YOU DON'T HAVE A SLOW COOKER...

At step 1 above, cook the 'slow cook' ingredients in a saucepan on the hob, with the lid on, over a medium heat for 25–35 minutes until the chicken is tender. Finish as above, returning the sweetcorn and shredded chicken to the pan for 5–10 minutes to heat through.

SLOW COOKER
BACON & LENTIL SOUP

3 HOURS 50 MINS

This is the stuff comfort food is made of. Warming and hearty, it also happens to be really affordable. I've left this soup very thick and rustic, but if you'd like something a little more elegant, add some extra water during or after cooking to thin it out a little more, you could also blend for a smooth soup.This soup also freezes very well. Pull out a portion for lunch and it will brighten up even the dreariest day.

1. **Put the slow cooker pot (if it's suitable for hob use) over a medium heat on the hob and add the oil. When the oil is hot, add the bacon pieces and cook for 5–10 minutes until starting to colour and turn golden. Add the onion, garlic, carrots, cumin, paprika, chilli flakes (if using) and some pepper and cook for a further 5 minutes until softened. If the slow cooker pot is not suitable for hob use, you'll need to use a sauté pan here.**

2. **Remove the pot from the heat and put into the slow cooker. Add the lentils, tinned tomatoes, tomato purée and stock. Give everything a good stir, pop the lid on and cook on HIGH for 3½– 4½ hours or LOW for 6–7 hours, until the lentils are very soft and the soup is thick. Ladle into bowls and serve with the bread for dunking.**

SERVES 4

1 tsp olive oil
250g smoked bacon, cut into small pieces (streaky or back bacon are both fine here)
1 onion, peeled and finely chopped
2 garlic cloves, peeled and crushed
2 carrots, peeled and chopped into very small pieces
2 tsp ground cumin
2 tsp sweet smoked paprika
¼ tsp dried chilli flakes (optional)
200g dried red lentils, rinsed
1 x 400g tin chopped tomatoes
2 tbsp tomato purée
1 litre hot vegetable stock (made with a stock cube is fine)
freshly ground black pepper

To Serve
crusty bread

When reheating this soup, you will almost certainly need to add a splash more water as it will become very thick when it cools.

Rinsing the lentils makes them less sticky and gloopy as they cook.

IF YOU DON'T HAVE A SLOW COOKER...

Fry the ingredients in a saucepan, as above, then at step 2 simmer on the hob over a medium heat, with the lid on, for 30–40 minutes until the lentils are soft and the soup is thick.

COMFORT FOOD

SLOW COOKER
CHICKEN STEW WITH PARMESAN DUMPLINGS

4 HOURS 45 MINS

Slow-cooker dumplings, are not quite like oven-baked, crunchy-topped dumplings, but are every bit as comforting. It's very hard to give an exact measurement for the water here as the flour you use, the heat of the butter and your hands can all make such a difference – just be sure to add the water a tiny bit at a time! It's important to use as little as possible or the dumplings can be a bit too wet.

1. Pan-fry the bacon over a high heat until crispy (if you have the type of slow cooker where the pot can be used on the hob, do this in the pot, otherwise you'll need to use a separate small frying pan or your sauté pan).

2. Put all of the slow cook ingredients, along with the crispy bacon and some salt and pepper, into the slow cooker pot, cover with the lid and cook on HIGH for 4–5 hours or LOW for 6–8 hours.

3. Around 15 minutes before the cooking time is up, make the dumplings. Put the flour in a large bowl and add the butter. Using clean hands, use a technique called 'rubbing in': put both hands into the bowl, lift up some of the butter with the flour mixture and rub between your thumb and fingers. Keep going and repeat until it all looks like lumpy sand. This will take about 5 minutes.

4. Add the Parmesan, oregano and some black pepper (you shouldn't need more salt as the Parmesan is quite salty) and mix. Add a small amount of cold water – start with 1 tablespoon – and mix with your hands, gently bringing the mixture together so it starts to form a ball. Add more water, a very small amount at a time, until the mixture just sticks together. Form into 8 small balls.

5. When the chicken is tender, use two forks to break it into large chunks. Sit the dumplings on the top of the stew. Place a clean tea towel over the top of the slow cooker, resting it across the edge of the dish (don't let it touch the dumplings) and put the lid on top of this. Cook for 30–45 minutes on HIGH, covered, until the dumplings are puffy and doubled in size.

SERVES 4

100g smoked bacon lardons
900g skinless, boneless chicken thighs
2 carrots, peeled and cut into 2cm pieces
2 leeks, trimmed and cut into 3cm pieces
500g new potatoes, cut into 3cm pieces
50g plain flour
650ml hot chicken stock (made from a stock cube is fine)
1 tbsp garlic granules
1 tbsp dried oregano
sea salt and freshly ground black pepper

For the Parmesan Dumplings
180g self-raising flour
100g salted butter, cold, cut into small cubes
30g Parmesan cheese, grated
1 tsp dried oregano
2–4 tbsp cold water

IF YOU DON'T HAVE A SLOW COOKER...

At the end of step 1, combine all the ingredients in a lidded casserole dish, cover and bake in the oven at 160°C fan/180°C/Gas Mark 4 for 30 minutes, then add the dumplings to the dish and cook with the lid on for 20 more minutes. Remove the lid and cook for a final 10 minutes.

HOT-HEADED COD

40 MINS / SERVE WITH LEMON COUSCOUS PAGE 146

Arrabiata means 'angry' in Italian, due to the fiery red pepper chillies traditionally used in the sauce of the same name. Here we've subdued the heat slightly with just a pinch of chilli flakes for some warmth, but nothing to scare off children and so, it's just hot headed, not quite angry.

1. **Heat the oil in a sauté pan over a high heat until very hot, then carefully add the peppers and onion. Cook for 5 minutes, or until they have just started to char and blacken at the edges, then turn the heat down to medium and add the garlic. Cook for 3–5 minutes until softened.**

2. **Add the tomatoes, chilli flakes and some salt and pepper and give everything a good stir. Pop the lid on and cook for 10 minutes.**

3. **Gently nestle the fish fillets into the sauce. Put the lid back on and cook over a medium heat for 14–18 minutes or until the fish is cooked through (see Notes).**

4. **Sprinkle over the basil, pushing some of it into the sauce if you can, then serve.**

SERVES 4

2 tbsp olive oil
3 red peppers, deseeded and cut into 1cm-thick strips
1 red onion, cut into 1cm-thick slices
4 garlic cloves, peeled and crushed
2 x 400g tins chopped tomatoes
pinch of dried chilli flakes
4 skinless cod fillets (about 500g in total) (see Notes)
15g fresh basil, finely shredded
sea salt and freshly ground black pepper

The heat of dried chilli flakes varies a lot. Start with just pinch and if you want to add more as the sauce cooks, you can.

Frozen fish fillets are almost always cheaper than fresh. Use frozen fish and adjust the cooking time according to the pack instructions (or defrost first if recommended on the pack). You could also use a cheaper white fish like basa.

The cooking time for fish fillets can vary a lot depending on their thickness: thinner fillets may cook more quickly and break up in the sauce if cooked for longer. Just check and keep an eye on them and remove from the heat when cooked through.

COMFORT FOOD

LEMON COUSCOUS
p.146

SLOW COOKER
LAMB & SPINACH CURRY

4 HOURS 20 MINS / **SERVE WITH TOMATO & ONION SALAD**

This recipe is a slow-cooker version of the favourite takeaway dish – sagwala. Traditionally the spinach is cooked and blended into a sauce, but here the slow cooking helps to break it down enough so that blending isn't needed. This recipe uses store-cupboard standbys of a jar of ready-made curry paste, tinned tomatoes, tinned chickpeas and some frozen spinach too. Serve this with naan, or roti for scooping.

1. **Put all of the slow cook ingredients into the slow cooker pot, cover with the lid and cook on HIGH for 4–5 hours or LOW for 6–7 hours.**

2. **Add the chickpeas, garam masala and mango chutney, replace the lid and cook on HIGH for a further 15–30 minutes until the chickpeas are hot through.**

SERVES 4

For the Slow Cook
450g diced lamb
1 onion, peeled and chopped
3 garlic cloves, peeled and crushed
1 x 400g tin chopped tomatoes
1 x 150g jalfrezi curry paste (not sauce)
½ tsp salt
2 lamb stock cubes (undiluted)
450g frozen spinach

To Finish
1 x 400g tin chickpeas, drained and rinsed
2 tsp garam masala
4 tbsp mango chutney

To Serve
naan or roti

TOMATO & ONION SALAD
(VG)

10 MINS / **SERVES 4**

4 salad tomatoes (about 350g in total), finely chopped
½ red onion, peeled and finely chopped
1 lemon, juiced
10g fresh mint, finely chopped
½ tsp sea salt

Mix all of the ingredients together in a bowl and serve immediately.

This recipe would be perfect for freezing as a Dump Bag (see page 17) – just freeze the 'slow cook' ingredients.

IF YOU DON'T HAVE A SLOW COOKER...
Cook the 'slow cook' ingredients in a lidded casserole dish in the oven at 160°C fan/180°C/Gas Mark 4 for 1½–2 hours, with an additional 100ml water. When the lamb is starting to feel very tender, add the remaining ingredients and return to the oven for 15–25 minutes until heated through.

COMFORT FOOD

TOMATO & ONION SALAD

BBQ SAUSAGE & BEAN BAKE

1 HOUR 10 MINS

This is baked beans, but not as we know it! Sausages and sweet potatoes are cooked all in one pan with the beans, coated in a speedy homemade barbecue sauce until sticky and sweet. Tasty, comforting and a complete meal on one tray. Don't be tempted to use regular white potatoes here, it doesn't quite work.

1. Preheat the oven to 200°C fan/220°C/Gas Mark 7.

2. Put the sweet potatoes and red onions on a baking tray, drizzle over the oil and add the paprika, garlic granules and plenty of salt and pepper. Toss well using a spoon, or even better, clean hands, to coat everything well. Sit the sausages on top.

3. Bake for 40 minutes or until just starting to turn golden.

4. Meanwhile, mix the sauce ingredients in a small bowl.

5. Remove the tray from the oven, flip the sausages, add the beans to the tray, pour over the sauce and sit the sweetcorn cobettes next to everything else. Bake for a final 20 minutes, until the corn is cooked through and the sauce is thick and sticky.

SERVES 4

1kg sweet potatoes (no need to peel), cut into 3cm chunks
2 red onions, peeled and cut into wedges
1 tbsp sunflower oil
2 tsp sweet smoked paprika
2 tsp garlic granules
450g pork sausages (or 8 sausages)
1 x 400g tin cannellini beans, drained and rinsed
4 sweetcorn cobettes
sea salt and freshly ground black pepper

For the Sauce
3 tbsp tomato ketchup
2 tbsp soft dark brown sugar
1 tsp white wine vinegar
1 tsp Dijon mustard

SLOW COOKER
MINTED LAMB STEW

5 HOURS 15 MINS

This comforting stew recipe would make a perfect Sunday lunch dish. As you know, if there's a shortcut, I will take it. But I have to say, I do think that we need to brown lamb for slow cooking. It not only gives extra flavour – which is needed when the meaty taste is the star of the show – but it also renders off some of the fat from the meat, which is often people's objection to lamb.

1. Put the slow cooker pot (if it's suitable for hob use) over a high heat on the hob. Pat the meat dry with some kitchen paper then add half the lamb (you don't want to overcrowd the pan). Fry for about 5 minutes, until browned all over. When it's browned, spoon it out onto a plate or bowl and repeat with the remaining lamb. (You won't need any oil as lamb is quite fatty.) If the slow cooker pot is not suitable for hob use, you'll need to use a sauté pan here.

2. Return the first batch of browned lamb to the pot, turn the heat down to low, add the flour and stir to coat the lamb. Turn off the heat and transfer the pot to your slow cooker. Add all the other ingredients, season with salt and pepper and give everything a good stir.

3. Pop the lid on and cook in the slow cooker on HIGH for 5–6 hours or on LOW for 8–9 hours (this will vary slightly depending on the size of the cubes of meat and vegetables but don't worry, it's difficult to overcook this.)

4. To serve, I add a final tablespoon of mint sauce – I like its freshness! Taste your stew and decide if you need it before adding.

SERVES 4

600g diced lamb
50g plain flour
1 onion, peeled and chopped
3 garlic cloves, peeled and crushed
4 carrots, peeled and cut into
   2cm pieces
750g new potatoes, halved
500ml hot lamb stock (made with
   a cube is fine)
3 tbsp Worcestershire sauce
   (or Henderson's Relish)
3 tbsp mint sauce (the vinegary
   type, not jelly)
sea salt and freshly ground
   black pepper

To Finish
1 tbsp mint sauce

IF YOU DON'T HAVE A SLOW COOKER...

At step 3 above, put the stew ingredients into a lidded casserole dish and cook the oven at 160°C fan/180°C/Gas Mark 4 for 2–3 hours until the lamb is tender (the cooking time will vary a lot depending on the size of the lamb cubes).

COMFORT FOOD

TURKEY TACO RICE

40 MINS

We love a tasty one-pot rice dish and a turkey taco; at some point they were destined to meet and live happily ever after. The level of spicing here should be fairly mild and suitable for children (unless you've bought a particularly fiery seasoning mix!), but if you'd like more heat, add another teaspoon or so.

1. **Heat the oil in a large sauté pan over a medium heat, add the turkey mince and cook for 5 minutes until starting to brown, breaking it up with a wooden spoon as it cooks.**

2. **Add the onion, garlic, peppers and fajita seasoning and cook for 5 minutes, until the vegetables start to soften, then add the rinsed rice to the pan with the tomato purée, black beans and stock. Season with salt and pepper and give everything a good stir. Pop the lid on and cook for 15–20 minutes, stirring occasionally, until the rice has absorbed all the stock.**

3. **Preheat the grill to high.**

4. **Fluff up the rice with a fork, add the cherry tomatoes and stir until combined. Sprinkle the cheese over the top and pop under the grill for 3–5 minutes until the cheese is just melted.**

SERVES 4

1 tbsp olive oil
500g turkey mince
1 onion, peeled and chopped
3 garlic cloves, peeled and crushed
3 peppers (whatever colour you prefer), deseeded and cut into 1cm pieces
4 tsp fajita seasoning
200g long-grain rice, rinsed
4 tbsp tomato purée
1 x 400g tin black beans, drained and rinsed
800ml hot chicken stock (made with a stock cube is fine)
100g cherry tomatoes, halved
75g grated mozzarella cheese
sea salt and freshly ground black pepper

I leave the cherry tomatoes uncooked in this as I think it gives a nice crunch. If you prefer yours softer, just add them to the rice 5 minutes before the end of the cooking time.

COMFORT FOOD

RED CURRY CHICKEN NOODLE SOUP

3 HOURS 40 MINS

This simple soup is inspired by Japanese ramen-style broths that my Manga-loving son adores. The chicken cooks gently in the soup base and then the noodles soak up that flavour. If you do fancy stretching to use another pan, a boiled or fried egg on top of this, while not necessary, is a tasty added extra.

1. **Put the slow cook ingredients into the slow cooker pot, pop the lid on and cook on HIGH for 3 hours or LOW for 5–6 hours.**

2. **When the timer has gone off and the chicken is cooked, remove the chicken from the broth to a plate or chopping board. Add the noodles, the stock and the sugar snap peas. Give everything a good stir and put the lid back on. Cook for 30 minutes on HIGH or until the noodles are soft.**

3. **Shred the chicken using two forks and keep it to one side to serve on top of the bowls of ramen after the noodles have finished cooking. (If you prefer the chicken to stay hot, you can shred it and add it back to the broth with the noodles as they cook.)**

4. **Add the lime juice. Serve topped with chilli oil if you fancy a bit more of a kick.**

SERVES 4

For the Slow Cook
300g skinless, boneless chicken breasts (or a pack of 2)
1 x 400ml tin reduced-fat coconut milk
200g chestnut mushrooms, cut into 1cm-thick slices
2 tbsp Thai red curry paste
75g smooth peanut butter
2 tbsp ginger purée (or fresh if you prefer)
3 garlic cloves, peeled and crushed
4 tbsp dark soy sauce (I use reduced salt)

To Finish
250g dried medium egg noodles
400ml hot vegetable stock (made with a stock cube is fine)
160g sugar snap peas
1 lime, juiced

To Serve
chilli oil (optional)

IF YOU DON'T HAVE A SLOW COOKER...
Put all of the 'slow cook' ingredients, plus 200ml of the vegetable stock, into a saucepan and simmer over a low to medium heat for 30–35 minutes until the chicken is cooked through. Remove the chicken, add the noodles, remaining stock and sugar snap peas, cover and cook for 10 minutes until the noodles and sugar snaps are cooked. Finish as above.

COMFORT FOOD

SLOW COOKER
PORK LETTUCE CUPS

5 HOURS / SERVE WITH PEANUT DIPPING SAUCE PAGE 146

Lettuce wraps or cups are found in lots of Asian cuisine, and almost all include some protein and a flavoursome sauce, piled into a leaf. Here I've added rice at the end of the cooking to make it more filling, but feel free to leave this out (you'd need to omit the stock too). If you've never used water chestnuts before, it's worth seeking out a tin; they add a satisfying crunch, while also adding some hidden veg (which is always a win as far as I'm concerned).

1. **Turn the mince out of its pack onto a plate and chop it with a sharp knife, this just helps to avoid big clumps forming as it cooks in the slow cooker.**

2. **Put the slow cook ingredients into the slow cooker pot, give everything a good stir and put the lid on. Cook on HIGH for 4–5 hours or LOW for 6–8 hours, until the pork is cooked through.**

3. **Add the rinsed rice, the stock, water chestnuts and soy sauce, give everything a good stir and put the lid back on. Cook for 45–60 minutes on HIGH or until the rice is cooked through.**

4. **Serve with the spring onions sprinkled on top and the lettuce leaves on the table ready to be filled up.**

SERVES 4

For the Slow Cook
500g pork mince (5% fat)
250g chestnut mushrooms, very finely chopped
4 garlic cloves, peeled and crushed
1 tbsp ginger purée (or fresh if you prefer)
3 tbsp oyster sauce
2 tsp Chinese 5-spice

To Finish
200g long-grain rice, rinsed
500ml hot vegetable stock (made with a stock cube is fine)
1 x 225g tin water chestnuts, drained, rinsed and cut into 1cm cubes
4 tbsp dark soy sauce (I use reduced salt)

To Serve
6 spring onions, finely chopped
2 or **3** small lettuces, I use little gem, leaves separated

IF YOU DON'T HAVE A SLOW COOKER...

Cook the 'slow cook' ingredients in a lidded saucepan on the hob over a high heat for 10 minutes until browned all over. Add the rice and stock and cook for 10–15 minutes until the rice is almost cooked and the liquid is absorbed (you may need to add a splash more water here if it looks dry), then add the water chestnuts and soy sauce and cook for 5 more minutes.

COMFORT FOOD

PEANUT
DIPPING
SAUCE
p.146

SIDES

PEANUT DIPPING SAUCE

5 MINS / SERVES 4

I call this a 'dipping sauce', but I could eat it straight from the spoon. It works so well with the lettuce cups on page 144 but also as a 'drizzle' on most dishes that use soy sauce.

80g smooth peanut butter
1 tbsp dark soy sauce (I use reduced salt)
1 tbsp sweet chilli sauce
2–6 tbsp boiling water

Put the peanut butter into a small bowl and add the soy sauce and sweet chilli sauce. Mix until combined (use a small whisk if you have one, or a fork).

Now add the boiling water, 1 tablespoon at a time. The sauce will look very split and, frankly, unpleasant to begin with but keep going – eventually it will come together.

Add more boiling water, a tablespoon at a time, until it's the consistency you prefer for dipping. The amount of water you need will vary a lot depending on the brand of peanut butter you use. Just keep going until it's a good saucy consistency.

LEMON COUSCOUS

15 MINS / SERVES 4

Couscous works so well with any stew or dish cooked in sauce, as it catches all of that flavour. Here we've kept this as a very simple side, with just a few flavours to add some zing.

320g couscous
400ml hot vegetable stock
(made with a stock cube is fine)
2 lemons, zested and juiced
2 tsp olive oil (extra-virgin olive oil if you have it)
15g fresh parsley, finely chopped
sea salt and freshly ground black pepper

Put the couscous and hot vegetable stock, along with the zest of the lemons, into a medium heatproof bowl. Mix well and cover the bowl with a plate.

Set aside for 10 minutes.

Uncover and use a fork to fluff up the couscous, add the juice of the lemons, the olive oil, fresh parsley and plenty of salt and pepper and mix well.

★

The stock here needs to be piping hot, made with just-boiled water, to be sure it will able to cook the couscous.

CORONATION COUSCOUS

15 MINS / SERVES 4

Couscous, that cooks simply as it sits in very hot stock, is a dream side dish. No faff. I buy a pre-chopped pack of mango for this recipe and just cut it up a little more, but feel free to prepare your own. You'll need the flesh of about half a single large mango.

320g couscous
150g frozen peas
400ml hot vegetable stock
(made with a stock cube is fine)
1 tsp mild curry powder
250g ripe mango, cut into 1cm cubes
(see above)
50g flaked almonds (toasted, if possible)
1 lemon, juiced
1 tbsp olive oil
sea salt and freshly ground black pepper

Put the couscous in a large bowl along with the frozen peas and add the hot vegetable stock and curry powder. Mix everything well and cover the bowl (I just use a dinner plate).

Set aside for 15 minutes or until the peas are defrosted and the couscous is cooked.

Remove the covering and use a fork to fluff up the couscous. Add the mango, flaked almonds, lemon juice, olive oil and plenty of salt and pepper. Mix well and serve.

The stock here needs to be piping hot, made with just-boiled water, to be sure it will able to cook the couscous.

SPOONFUL SALAD

10 MINS / SERVES 4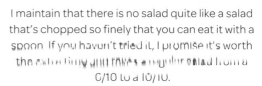

I maintain that there is no salad quite like a salad that's chopped so finely that you can eat it with a spoon. If you haven't tried it, I promise it's worth the extra time and takes a regular salad from a 6/10 to a 10/10.

1 lettuce (I like cos or romaine), very finely chopped
2 salad tomatoes, very finely chopped
½ red onion, very finely chopped
½ cucumber, very finely chopped

For the dressing
2 tbsp olive oil (extra-virgin if you have it)
2 tbsp white wine vinegar
¼ tsp sea salt

Make the dressing by whisking the ingredients together until smooth, or I prefer to pop them into a clean jar and shake very hard. This gives a better result as the fats in the oil become extra creamy.

Add the salad ingredients to a serving bowl, pour the dressing over just before serving, then toss well.

Use extra-virgin olive oil if you have it; if you don't, regular olive oil also works, but just won't be quite as flavourful.

SLOW COOKER
PORK CHILLI

5 HOURS 40 MINS / SERVE WITH SPICY CORN SALAD

Using pork for a chilli recipe makes a tasty change from the usual beef mince. Up the chilli quota if you're braver than my children. This is one of the few recipes in this book that isn't a complete meal straight from the pan, but honestly, it was too good like this to change it and add anything else. How about serving it over some nachos, with melted cheese on top? Or in a burrito, as a topping for a baked potato, or with some rice and guacamole?

1. **Use a sharp knife to carefully cut the skin and some of the fat layer off the pork. Discard the skin.**

2. **Put all of the slow cook ingredients into the slow cooker pot, season with salt and pepper, put the lid on and cook on HIGH for 5–7 hours or LOW for 9–11 hours.**

3. **When the pork is very tender, shred it with two forks (I like to remove it from the slow cooker to a plate to do this as it's much easier). You can discard any fatty lumps now if you like. Return the shredded pork to the slow cooker.**

4. **Add the black beans, give everything a good stir and put the lid back on. Cook on HIGH for a further 30 minutes, until the beans are hot.**

SPICY CORN SALAD

10 MINS / SERVES 4

Turn a storecupboard tin of sweetcorn into something special.

1 x 325g tin sweetcorn, drained
½ red onion, peeled and finely chopped
1 lime, juiced
1 tbsp olive oil (extra-virgin if you have it)
pinch of dried chilli flakes
½ tsp ground cumin
¼ tsp sea salt

Mix all the ingredients together in a bowl and serve.

SERVES 4

For the Slow Cook
1.5kg pork shoulder (see Notes)
75g tomato purée
500g passata
4 tsp ground cumin
1 tbsp mild chilli powder
1 tbsp dried oregano
4 tsp garlic granules
2 tbsp soft dark brown sugar
sea salt and freshly ground
    black pepper

To Finish
1 x 400g tin black beans, drained
    and rinsed

To Serve
microwave rice, wraps or nachos

★

The cooking time here can vary a lot depending on the shape of the piece of pork. It's difficult to overcook this though, so I'd always allow more cooking time rather than less in case it isn't quite cooked when you check it.

★

Although most supermarkets sell pork shoulder in a 1.5kg pack size, I do cut off a good layer of fat before slow cooking as it's just not needed. The piece you'll end up cooking is usually more like 1.2kg.

SPICY CORN SALAD

IF YOU DON'T HAVE A SLOW COOKER...
At step 2, add an additional 150ml water and cook in the oven, in a lidded casserole dish, at
150°C fan/170°C/Gas Mark 3 for 5–6 hours until the pork is very tender. At step 4, return to the oven
for the 30 minutes to heat the beans.

UPSIDE-DOWN LOADED NACHOS

5 HOURS 50 MINS

Of all the recipes in this book, we've probably eaten this one more than any other, as it needed plenty of tweaking to get it right, but oh boy, it was worth the effort. Easy, satisfying and topped with tortilla chips – what more could you want?! To make a vegetarian version, replace the mince with an additional tin of drained beans and replace the beef stock with a vegetarian alternative.

SERVES 4

1. **Put all the slow cook ingredients into the slow cooker pot, season with salt and pepper, stir well, put the lid on and cook on HIGH for 5–6 hours or LOW for 8–10 hours, or until the sauce is thick and rich.**

2. **Add the pepper chunks, rinsed rice and beef stock. Give everything a good stir, put the lid back on and cook for 45–60 minutes on HIGH, until the rice is cooked.**

3. **Now you have two options:**

   a) Sprinkle the cheese over the meat and rice, put the lid back on and cook on HIGH for 5–10 minutes until the cheese is melted. Top with the tortilla chips and serve.

   OR

   b) If your slow cooker pan is grill/oven safe, sprinkle the tortilla chips on top, add the grated cheese and pop under a hot grill for 5 minutes to melt the cheese and crisp the tortilla chips. Watch carefully as they can burn very quickly.

For the Slow Cook
500g beef mince (5% fat)
1 onion, peeled and finely chopped
1 x 400g tin chopped tomatoes
1 x 400g tin kidney beans, drained and rinsed
75g tomato purée
2 tsp ground cumin
2 tsp dried oregano
2 tsp paprika
1 tsp mild chilli powder
1 tbsp garlic granules
1 tbsp Worcestershire sauce (or Henderson's Relish)
sea salt and freshly ground black pepper

To Finish
1 green pepper, deseeded and cut into 2cm chunks
150g long-grain rice, rinsed
350ml hot beef stock (made with a stock cube is fine)
100g tortilla chips
100g grated mozzarella cheese

IF YOU DON'T HAVE A SLOW COOKER...

Cook the 'slow cook' ingredients in a sauté pan on the hob over a medium heat for 25–30 minutes until thickened (you may need to add a splash of water if it starts to dry out). Add the peppers, rice and stock, cover and cook for a further 10–15 minutes until the rice is almost cooked and the liquid is absorbed (you may need to add a splash more water here if it looks dry). Add the tortilla chips and cheese and finish as above.

SLOW COOKER
HONEY & MUSTARD PORK

5 HOURS 25 MINS

I use a pork fillet here, cut into bite-sized pieces, as I find that pork shoulder or other cuts in a casserole need browning first as they are quite fatty. Using a fillet is a way of avoiding needing to brown anything (hurrah!) and reducing the fat content (if that's something that bothers you).

1. **Put all the slow cook ingredients into the slow cooker pot, season with salt and pepper and put the lid on. Cook for HIGH for 5 hours or LOW for 7–8 hours.**

2. **When the timer is up and the potatoes are cooked through, put the cornflour in a small bowl and add a little of the milk at a time, whisking until you get a smooth paste. Add the paste to the slow cooker, then add the honey and give everything a good stir. Put the lid back on and cook for a further 15 minutes on HIGH.**

For the Slow Cook
1 pork fillet, also known as tenderloin (usually about 500g), cut into 3cm pieces
750g new potatoes, cut into 3cm pieces
3 leeks (about 500g), trimmed and cut into 1cm rounds
3 carrots, peeled and cut into 2cm pieces
500ml hot vegetable stock (made with a stock cube is fine)
2 tsp wholegrain mustard
1 tsp dried parsley
sea salt and freshly ground black pepper

To Finish
30g cornflour
100ml milk (semi-skimmed or full-fat)
2 tbsp runny honey

This recipe would be perfect for freezing as a Dump Bag (see page 17). Freeze the 'slow cook' ingredients, minus the stock. Defrost and continue to cook as per the recipe.

IF YOU DON'T HAVE A SLOW COOKER...

Cook in a saucepan on the hob, with the lid on, for 1–1½ hours over a low heat. Finish with the cornflour, milk and honey as per the recipe above, cooking for an additional 15–20 minutes.

COMFORT FOOD

SLOW COOKER
CHORIZO & BEAN STEW

The flavours from the chorizo here turn some humble (and affordable!) tinned beans into a rich, fragrant stew. Don't be put off by the sugar here, it helps to balance the slightly tart tomatoes. Serve with plenty of crusty bread for dunking.

1. **Pan-fry the chorizo on the hob, over a high heat for about 5 minutes until the chunks are starting to go crispy. You won't need any oil here as the chorizo will release plenty as it cooks. (If the slow cooker pot is not suitable for hob use, you'll need to use a sauté pan here.)**

2. **Add the onion, garlic and carrots and fry for a further 5 minutes until the onion has softened.**

3. **Turn off the heat, return the pot to the slow cooker (or tip the contents of the sauté pan into the slow cooker pot) and add all of the other ingredients, seasoning with salt and pepper.**

4. **Cover with the lid and cook on HIGH for 5–6 hours or LOW for 8–10 hours until the stew is thick and rich. Spoon into bowls and serve.**

SERVES 4

200g chorizo (the type in a ring), cut into 1cm chunks
1 onion, peeled and chopped
3 garlic cloves, peeled and crushed
2 carrots, peeled and chopped into 2cm pieces
2 x 400g tins chopped tomatoes
1 x 400g tin butter beans, drained and rinsed
1 x 400g tin chickpeas, drained and rinsed
1 x 400g tin cannellini beans, drained and rinsed
1 tbsp sweet smoked paprika
1 tbsp soft dark brown sugar
2 tbsp tomato purée
150ml water
1 vegetable stock cube (undiluted)
sea salt and freshly ground black pepper

To Serve
crusty bread

IF YOU DON'T HAVE A SLOW COOKER...

Follow steps 1 and 2 as above, in a lidded casserole dish, then add the remaining ingredients and cook, with a lid on, over a low heat for a further 25–30 minutes until the sauce is rich and thick.

SPANISH-ISH CHICKEN & CHORIZO RICE

40 MINS

This recipe is something vaguely in the direction of a paella (hence the name!). The chorizo and paprika add colour and flavour as the rice cooks in the stock, all in one pan. Don't forget the good squeeze of lemon before serving – it makes the dish.

1. Heat a sauté pan over a medium heat and add the chorizo pieces. Fry for 3–5 minutes until the oil begins to release from the chorizo into the pan.

2. Add the chicken pieces and continue to fry for 5 minutes, then turn the heat up to high and add the onion, garlic, pepper strips and paprika and fry for another 5 minutes until the vegetables are starting to colour.

3. Turn the heat down to medium, add the rinsed rice, tomato purée, stock and plenty of salt and pepper. Give everything a good stir, pop the lid on, and cook for 15 minutes.

4. Add the peas, cover and cook for a further 3–5 minutes until the peas are cooked and almost all of the liquid is absorbed.

5. Serve with the lemon quarters to squeeze over.

SERVES 4

200g chorizo (the type in a ring), cut into 1cm-thick rounds
650g skinless, boneless chicken thighs, cut into bite-sized pieces
1 onion, peeled and chopped
3 garlic cloves, peeled and crushed
3 red peppers, deseeded and cut into 2cm-thick strips
4 tsp paprika
200g long-grain rice, rinsed
4 tbsp tomato purée
800ml hot chicken stock (made with a stock cube is fine)
200g frozen peas
sea salt and freshly ground black pepper

To Serve
2 lemons, quartered

SLOW COOKER
SPICED ROAST CHICKEN

5 HOURS 15 MINS / SERVE WITH CORONATION COUSCOUS PAGE 147

Slow cooking a whole chicken is not only easy, but very effective as the meat is less likely to be dry, and there's no need to switch the whole oven on. The skin won't be crispy like a traditional roast chicken, but you can pop it under the grill to achieve this at the end of the cooking process. If you are nearby as this recipe cooks, start the chicken upside down (breasts facing down) and then flip it over after 2 hours cooking for the remaining time. This will keep the meat even more tender.

SERVES 4

For the Slow Cook
1 whole chicken (about 1.5kg)
100ml water

For the Spice Paste
1 tbsp ground cumin
1 tbsp paprika
2 tsp garlic granules
1 tsp ground turmeric
4 tbsp sunflower oil
sea salt and freshly ground
    black pepper

1. **Sit your unwrapped chicken in the slow cooker pot and carefully cut some 'slashes' across each breast, through the skin but not too deep, about 1cm. (This allows the flavour of the spice paste to get into the chicken breasts.)**

2. **Mix the paste ingredients together in a small bowl and use a brush or clean hands to coat the chicken all over with it. Rub it into all of the nooks and crannies, including the slashes you cut into the breasts. Season with plenty of salt and pepper.**

3. **Sit the chicken, breasts facing upwards, into the slow cooker (facing them downwards if you are able to flip it after 2 hours – see introduction above). Pour 100ml water into the base of the slow cooker pot, around the chicken.**

4. **Put the lid on and cook on LOW for 5–5½ hours. Check the chicken is cooked by inserting a meat thermometer into the thickest part of the chicken. If you don't have a thermometer, it will be ready when a chicken leg easily pulls away and the juices from the thickest part of the meat run clear.**

5. **When the chicken is cooked, preheat the grill to HIGH. Put it onto a grill-proof dish and cook for about 10 minutes until the skin is crispy and golden. (You can leave out this step and serve the chicken straight from the slow cooker, but the soft skin does not look very appealing!)**

IF YOU DON'T HAVE A SLOW COOKER...
You can use this spice rub on any regular chicken, roasted in the oven.

COMFORT FOOD

CORONATION COUSCOUS
p.147

SMOKY RED FRITTATA

40 MINS / SERVE WITH SPOONFUL SALAD PAGE 147

Frying humble potatoes in chorizo juices is a sure-fire way to transform them. They become red and smoky, little flavour sponges that make this easy dish more than the sum of its parts. Leftovers make a wonderful lunch, and you can add in any other vegetables you fancy. I've kept it simple here with tomatoes as I love the colour. Peas or courgettes work well too. Also, I can never get enough of cheese, so if you have some hanging around looking for a good home, it wouldn't go amiss on top here.

1. **Heat a sauté pan over a medium heat, add the chorizo and fry for 5 minutes until it just starts to colour and has released its oil.**

2. **Add the potato cubes, give everything a good stir, put the lid on the pan and cook for 15–20 minutes, stirring occasionally, until the potatoes are cooked through. (See Notes)**

3. **Add the tomatoes and a generous helping of salt and pepper, give everything a good stir, then turn the heat down to low and pour over the eggs. Leave the lid off the pan and cook for 10 minutes until you can see the edges of the frittata beginning to set.**

4. **Preheat the grill to high.**

5. **Pop the frittata under the grill for about 5 minutes to finish it off. It's cooked when the top is set and golden, and if you prod the middle with a knife there's no liquid egg.**

SERVES 4

200g chorizo (the type in a ring), cut into 2cm chunks
600g white potatoes, I like Maris Piper or King Edward, cut into 2cm cubes (no need to peel)
200g frozen peas
200g cherry tomatoes
6 eggs, lightly beaten
sea salt and freshly ground black pepper

As your potatoes cook in the pan in step 2, keep an eye on them. If you aren't using a reliably non-stick pan, they may stick, in which case your options are; turn the heat down a little to cook them for longer but more slowly and/or add a splash of water to stop the potatoes sticking. If I'm using a less than ideal pan, I'd definitely do both to be on the safe side.

COMFORT FOOD

SPOONFUL SALAD
p.147

SATAY-STYLE BRAISED BEEF

5 HOURS 10 MINS

In this recipe the beef is braised slowly in coconut milk with spices and a dollop of peanut butter. The result is a silky-smooth curried sauce. The tomatoes added at the end give it a pop of freshness and colour. Serve with flatbreads or rice (microwave rice to keep this a one-pot meal!).

1. **Put the beef in the slow cooker pot with the flour and stir well to coat the meat.**

2. **Add all the other slow cook ingredients and mix well, put the lid on and cook on HIGH for 5–6 hours or LOW for 8–10 hours, or until the beef is tender.**

3. **Before serving, add the tomatoes and stir well. Serve with the peanuts sprinkled over.**

SERVES 4

For the Slow Cook
700g diced beef
40g plain flour
4 garlic cloves, peeled and crushed
1 tbsp ginger purée (or use fresh if you prefer)
1 x 400ml tin reduced-fat coconut milk
4 tbsp dark soy sauce (I used reduced salt)
4 tsp mild curry powder
250g chestnut mushrooms, halved
50g peanut butter (crunchy or smooth are fine)

To Serve
200g cherry tomatoes, halved
75g salted peanuts
flatbreads or microwave rice

This recipe is perfect for freezing as a Dump Bag (see page 17). Just omit the coconut milk from the bag and defrost and add to the contents as per the recipe, before cooking.

IF YOU DON'T HAVE A SLOW COOKER...

Coat the beef in the flour, as above, then add all of the 'slow cook' ingredients to a lidded casserole dish and cook at 160°C fan/180°C/Gas Mark 4 for 2½– 3½ hours, or until the beef is tender, along with an additional 200ml beef stock. Finish as per the recipe above.

COMFORT FOOD

SPEEDY SUPPERS

THAI-STYLE RED RICE

35 MINS

I've only recently embraced the absolute flavour bomb that is red Thai curry paste. It's so useful for adding lots of flavour to one-pot dishes quickly, although I've noticed that it can vary a lot in heat by brand. Be mindful of this, and if you are very concerned with any warmth or are using a paste you haven't used before, perhaps start with 2 tablespoons instead of 3 tablespoons.

1 tsp sunflower oil
500g beef mince (5% fat)
3 tbsp Thai red curry paste (see above)
4 garlic cloves, peeled and crushed
200g long-grain rice, rinsed
1 x 400ml tin reduced-fat coconut milk
300–400ml hot vegetable stock (made with a stock cube is fine)
2 red peppers, deseeded and cut into 2cm pieces
200g baby corn, cut into 1cm-thick rounds
sea salt

To Serve
2 limes, quartered

1. Heat the oil in a sauté pan over a high heat, add the mince and fry for 5–10 minutes until browned all over, breaking it up with a wooden spoon as it browns.

2. Turn the heat down to medium and add the curry paste and garlic. Cook for 5 minutes, stirring so that the paste doesn't stick, then add the rinsed rice, coconut milk, 300ml of the stock and a good pinch of sea salt. Give everything a thorough stir, put the lid on and cook for 10 minutes.

3. Add the peppers and baby corn, cover and cook for a further 8–10 minutes, until the rice is cooked, the vegetables are tender and the liquid is absorbed. If your mixture is looking quite dry, add the remaining 100ml of the stock – if it still looks quite wet, it's not needed.

4. When everything is cooked, serve with the lime quarters on the side for squeezing.

PRAWN & PEA ORZO

30 MINS

When cooking orzo in a pan with stock, you end up with something like a risotto but without the constant stirring and attention required. Perfect for a midweek dinner. Here I've added some garlic and herb cream cheese before serving as a tasty shortcut. You can use fresh, cooked prawns if you prefer – just reduce the cooking time slightly.

1. Heat the oil in a sauté pan over a medium heat. Add the onion and garlic and cook for 4–5 minutes until just starting to soften.

2. Add the orzo, stock and the zest of the lemon (save the rest for the end of the cooking time), along with a good grind of black pepper.

3. Cover the pan and cook for 10 minutes, stirring occasionally.

4. Turn the heat down to low and add the prawns, long-stemmed broccoli and peas and stir everything together well. Put the lid back on and cook for a further 8–10 minutes.

5. Remove the pan from the heat. Check that the prawns have turned pink throughout (a sign they are cooked) and check for seasoning. Add some salt if needed (you may not need any as stock can be salty enough). Stir in the juice of the lemon and the cream cheese, continue to stir until the cream cheese has melted and serve immediately.

SERVES 4

2 tsp olive oil
1 onion, peeled and chopped
3 garlic cloves, peeled and crushed
250g orzo (uncooked)
800ml hot vegetable stock
(made with a stock cube is fine)
1 lemon, zested and juiced
300g frozen raw peeled king prawns
200g long-stemmed broccoli,
cut into 4cm lengths
200g frozen peas
200g garlic and herb cream cheese
sea salt and freshly ground
black pepper

FANCY FISH FINGER SANDWICHES

25 MINS / SERVE WITH MINTED PEA SALAD PAGE 175

A fish finger sandwich is one of my ultimate treat foods and this homemade version takes it to a new level of fancy, which I am very much here for. There will always be a place in my heart for fluorescent orange fish fingers from the freezer, but it has to be said, this is a little more impressive.

1. Preheat the oven to 180°C fan/200°C/Gas Mark 6.

2. Put the fish fillet chunks on a plate and blot them with some kitchen paper to dry the surface.

3. In a shallow bowl, mix the breadcrumbs, lemon zest (save the rest of the lemon for later), parsley and plenty of salt and pepper.

4. Put the beaten egg in a shallow bowl. Dunk each fish fillet chunk into the egg, then roll in the seasoned breadcrumbs to coat.

5. Sit the breaded fish on a baking tray, drizzle with the oil and bake in the oven for 10 minutes until starting to turn golden.

6. While they are cooking, mix the sauce ingredients in a bowl. Add a little squeeze of juice from the leftover lemon. Taste the sauce and add more of the juice until you're happy with the flavour.

7. Add the burger bun halves to the baking tray and cook for a further 5 minutes, until the fish pieces are cooked and the bread is lightly toasted.

8. Rest a slice of cheese on each of the 4 burger bun bases and cook for 1–2 minutes more until the cheese is softened.

9. Pile up the buns with the sauce, shredded lettuce and coated fish pieces.

SERVES 4

400g skinless cod fillets, cut into big chunks (see Notes)
75g dried breadcrumbs, such as panko
1 lemon, zest and juice
1 tsp dried parsley
1 egg, beaten
1 tbsp olive oil
sea salt and freshly ground black pepper

For the Sauce
50g mayonnaise
50g Greek yoghurt
2 gherkins, finely chopped
1 tsp dried parsley

To Serve
4 burger buns (like brioche)
4 slices Cheddar cheese
2 little gem lettuces, shredded

Try to cut the fish into similar-sized pieces so they cook evenly. We cut them like this rather than serving in whole fillets, so you get a better crispy outside-crumb-to-fish ratio!

You can use any white fish you prefer. You can also use frozen and defrosted fish.

MINTED PEA SALAD

p.175

ZESTY CHICKEN PILAF

35 MINS

This finished dish looks so pretty when served in your sauté pan, with the pretty slices of lemon on top, no one would guess how simple it is! If you like it even more zesty (I do) use two lemons instead of one. Frozen green beans work well here if you prefer them to fresh; they are often cheaper.

SERVES 4

1 tbsp olive oil
4 skinless, boneless chicken breasts (about 650g in total)
1 onion, peeled and thinly sliced
4 garlic cloves, peeled and crushed
200g long-grain rice, rinsed
650ml hot chicken stock (made with a stock cube is fine)
2 tsp dried oregano
200g green beans, trimmed and cut in half
150g baby spinach
1 lemon, cut into 4 thick slices
sea salt and freshly ground black pepper

1. Heat the oil in a sauté pan over a medium heat. Add the chicken breasts, put the lid on and cook for 5–10 minutes, until the side touching the pan is golden brown: there's no need to flip the chicken over, we are browning on one side only.

2. Remove the chicken from the pan and transfer to a plate. Add the onion and garlic to the same pan (no need to clean it) and cook for 3–5 minutes until softened.

3. Add the rinsed rice, stock, oregano and plenty of salt and pepper to the pan. Give everything a good stir, put the lid back on and cook for 5 minutes.

4. Take off the lid, add the green beans and spinach and give everything a good stir. Sit the chicken breasts back into the pan, with the browned side facing up. Place the slices of lemon on and around the chicken.

5. Pop the lid on and cook for 10–15 minutes over a medium heat, stirring occasionally, until the chicken is cooked through, the beans are tender, the rice is cooked and the liquid has been absorbed.

TRAFFIC-LIGHT PIZZA

30 MINS / SERVE WITH CAESAR-ISH SALAD PAGE 174

Making a homemade pizza on a weeknight would 100 per cent not normally be my style, but this is ready in about half an hour using a nifty, no-yeast dough. You can obviously use whatever toppings you fancy, but I like to sneak in some extra vegetables wherever I can. If the dough sticks a bit as you roll it out, don't worry too much – it's very forgiving, you can just squish it back together.

1. Preheat the oven to 200°C fan/220°C/Gas Mark 7 and put an empty baking tray into the oven to get hot too.

2. In a large bowl mix the flour, Greek yoghurt and salt until they come together to form a ball. Use clean hands to knead the mixture for 5 minutes until it is smooth and a little springy. Set aside.

3. Put all the sauce ingredients in a small bowl and mix together.

4. Lay a sheet of baking paper on the work surface, sprinkle it with a little extra flour and turn the dough out onto it. Use a rolling pin (or your hands, or a clean wine bottle) to carefully roll the dough out to fit your baking tray. You will almost certainly need to sprinkle the rolling pin with a little extra flour to stop it sticking. The thinner you can roll it the better.

5. Spread the sauce over the top of the pizza base. Add the sweetcorn, cheese and cherry tomatoes, then spoon over the pesto in little dollops.

6. Bake for 15–20 minutes until golden and crisp, then slice and serve.

SERVES 4

400g self-raising flour, plus extra for dusting
400g full-fat Greek yoghurt
1 tsp sea salt
100g tinned sweetcorn, drained (see Notes)
150g grated mozzarella cheese
100g cherry tomatoes, halved
2 tsp green pesto

For the Sauce
150g passata (see Notes)
2 tsp garlic granules
1 tsp dried oregano
sea salt and freshly ground black pepper

I'm very cross that this recipe uses only part of a tin of sweetcorn and part of a carton of passata. I always try and avoid this in recipes as I know how frustrating these leftovers can be. Unfortunately, here it was unavoidable. For the sweetcorn, serve the rest of the tin on the side of the pizza or as an extra vegetable side with any other dinner. For the passata, you could add this to any other more 'saucy' tomato dish or use as an instant pasta sauce for another day.

I prefer to use grated mozzarella cheese here, rather than the fresh-style balls, as they can sometimes be a little too watery for this dough.

CAESAR-ISH SALAD
p.174

SIDES

SPEEDY AVOCADO SALSA

5 MINS / SERVES 4

This quick salad is an easy way of adding some instant fresh veg and colour to your meal, without turning to a bag of lettuce leaves.
Add some dried chilli flakes if you're that way inclined.

2 avocados, halved, peeled, stone removed and cut into 2cm cubes
½ red onion, peeled and cut into 1cm cubes
150g cherry tomatoes, halved
1 tbsp olive oil (extra-virgin if you have it)
½ tsp sea salt

Mix the ingredients together in a bowl and serve.

CAESAR-ISH SALAD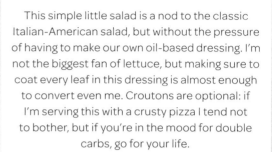

10 MINS / SERVES 4

This simple little salad is a nod to the classic Italian-American salad, but without the pressure of having to make our own oil-based dressing. I'm not the biggest fan of lettuce, but making sure to coat every leaf in this dressing is almost enough to convert even me. Croutons are optional: if I'm serving this with a crusty pizza I tend not to bother, but if you're in the mood for double carbs, go for your life.

1 cos or romaine lettuce, cut into 3cm pieces
50g Parmesan cheese, grated (see Notes)
50g croutons (optional)

For the Dressing
100g mayonnaise
1 garlic clove, peeled and crushed
2 tbsp white wine vinegar
1 tsp Dijon mustard
sea salt and freshly ground black pepper

Mix the dressing ingredients in a small bowl until smooth and well combined.

Put the lettuce leaves in a bowl and add the dressing, toss well using a spoon (or clean hands) until everything is well coated.

Serve sprinkled with grated Parmesan cheese and croutons (if using).

I like to 'peel' the cheese for this recipe, using a vegetable peeler to make curly strips. It makes it feel a little bit fancy.

SESAME & GINGER SLAW

10 MINS / SERVES 4

The bright colours and warming dressing of this salad are enough to tempt even vegetable haters to try it. Don't forget the sesame seeds, they add both texture and flavour.

½ white cabbage, finely shredded
2 red peppers, deseeded and thinly sliced
1 red onion, peeled and thinly sliced
4 tbsp olive oil
2 tbsp runny honey
2 tbsp white wine vinegar
1 tsp ginger purée (see Notes)
½ tsp sea salt
freshly ground black pepper
2 tbsp white sesame seeds, to serve

Put all the ingredients apart from the sesame seeds, into a large bowl and mix until fully coated.

Sprinkle over the sesame seeds before serving.

If you have fresh ginger to hand, swap the ginger purée for freshly grated ginger.

MINTED PEA SALAD

20 MINS / SERVES 4

Did you know you could cook peas without cooking peas?! Just leave them in freshly boiled water and they will defrost and give you the base for a tasty salad, with it maybe a happy change from lettuce.

300g frozen peas
100g feta cheese, crumbled (optional)

For the Dressing
1 lemon, zested and juiced
2 tbsp olive oil
1 garlic clove, peeled and crushed
15g fresh mint, very finely chopped
sea salt and freshly ground black pepper

Put the peas in a large heatproof bowl and cover with boiling water.
Set aside for 15 minutes until they are defrosted.

Mix all the dressing ingredients together in a bowl.

When the peas are defrosted, drain and toss with the dressing.

Crumble over the feta (if using).

TURKEY & LIME BURGERS

25 MINS / SERVE WITH SESAME & GINGER SLAW PAGE 175

These simple burgers make a tasty change from a usual beef burger and the zesty lime is a quick shortcut, which adds flavour. You may want to leave the chilli jam out if cooking these for young children, but if you can, please use it: it keeps the burgers tender and adds a very subtle kick.

1. Using clean hands, mix the burger ingredients in a bowl with some salt and pepper until fully combined, then shape into 4 even-sized burgers.

2. Heat the olive oil in a sauté pan over a medium heat. Add the burgers and cook for 7– 8 minutes on each side. If you feel like the burgers are browning too much (aka burning!) turn the heat down to low and put the lid on the pan – this will slow down the cooking and avoid them colouring too much on the outside.

3. While the burgers are cooking, mix the sauce ingredients together in a bowl.

4. When the burgers are golden on the outside and cooked through, serve them in the toasted buns, topped with the lettuce and the sauce.

SERVES 4

For the Burgers
500g turkey mince
1 egg
30g dried breadcrumbs, such as panko
4 tsp chilli jam
2 limes, zested (save the juice for the sauce)
1 tsp garlic granules
1 tsp onion powder
sea salt and freshly ground black pepper

For the Sauce
60g mayonnaise
60g Greek yoghurt
1 tbsp chilli jam
juice of the 2 limes

To Cook and Serve
2 tsp olive oil
4 burger buns, such as brioche, split in half and toasted
2 little gem lettuces, leaves separated

SESAME & GINGER SLAW
p 175

POLLO PESTO RICE

35 MINS

A well-known restaurant chain features a pasta dish with the same name as this. It's been a regular order of mine forever, so I thought I should probably mix it up a little at home and came up with this rice version. It's simple, tasty and super comforting. The creamy, cheesy rice feels something like a risotto, without the delicate cooking method.

1. Heat the oil in a large sauté pan over a medium heat. When the oil is hot add the chicken and cook for about 5 minutes, stirring occasionally, until sealed all over and starting to colour.

2. Add the onion, garlic, mushrooms and some salt and pepper, then turn the heat to high and cook for 5 minutes, until the vegetables start to soften.

3. Add the rinsed rice, stock and pesto to the pan. Give everything a good stir. Once the liquid has started to bubble place the lid on, reduce the heat to medium and cook for 10 minutes, stirring occasionally.

4. Add the peas, cover and cook for a further 5 minutes.

5. Once the rinsed rice is soft and the chicken is cooked through, turn off the heat and add the mozzarella. Give everything a good stir until combined and the cheese just begins to melt, then serve.

SERVES 4

1 tbsp olive oil
650g skinless, boneless chicken breasts, cut into small chunks
1 red onion, peeled and sliced.
3 garlic cloves, peeled and crushed
400g chestnut mushrooms, sliced
200g long-grain rice, rinsed
800ml hot chicken stock (made with a stock cube is fine)
100g green pesto
200g frozen peas
125g buffalo mozzarella, drained and cut into small cubes
sea salt and freshly ground black pepper

CHEESY BEAN TORTILLA ROLLS

20 MINS / SERVE WITH SPEEDY AVOCADO SALSA PAGE 174

This speedy supper is a firm favourite in our house. It's something like Mexican taquitos, but oven-baked rather than crispy fried. I recommend using wholemeal wraps here, not only for the nutrients, but because they also tend to get crispier in the oven than standard ones.

1. Preheat the oven to 180°C fan/200°C/Gas Mark 6.

2. Put the black beans, cannellini beans, sweetcorn, red onion, both containers of salsa, the fajita seasoning and a generous pinch of salt and pepper in a large bowl and mix well.

3. Lay the wraps out and use 150g of the cheese to sprinkle a line along the middle of each one, then share the filling out between each one, on top of the cheese, in a thin line.

4. Roll up each tortilla tightly in a sausage shape and lay them in a baking tray in a row, pushing them next to each other to stop them from unravelling.

5. Sprinkle the remaining cheese in a line along the middle of the tortilla rolls.

6. Drizzle the oil over the parts of the tortilla rolls you can see and bake in the oven for 10–15 minutes until the cheese is melted and the edges of the wraps are crispy.

7. While everything is cooking mix the dressing together in a small bowl.

8. Serve with the dressing drizzled over.

SERVES 4

1 x 400g tin black beans, drained and rinsed
1 x 400g tin cannellini beans, drained and rinsed
1 x 200g tin sweetcorn, drained
1 red onion, peeled and very finely chopped
2 x 200g containers fresh tomato salsa (from the supermarket dips aisle)
1 tbsp fajita seasoning
8 wholegrain tortilla wraps
250g grated mozzarella cheese
2 tsp sunflower oil
sea salt and freshly ground black pepper

For the Dressing
60g mayonnaise
1 lime, zested and juiced

SPEEDY AVOCADO SALSA
p.171

SPEEDY GINGER PORK STIR-FRY

25 MINS

This trick of throwing pouches of ready-cooked rice into a pan saves me so often when I'm staring at a pan wondering what to rustle up for dinner. A quick sauce here infuses the rice with heaps of flavour and the cashew nuts on top add texture.

1. Heat the oil in a sauté pan over a high heat and add the pork mince. Cook for 5 minutes, until browned all over, using a wooden spoon to break up the mince as it cooks.

2. Meanwhile, combine the sauce ingredients in a small bowl and set side.

3. Add the ginger purée, garlic, Chinese 5-spice and baby corn to the pork and cook for a further 2–3 minutes until the corn is just starting to colour.

4. Add the rice to the pan (no need to preheat it). (These microwave rice pouches can be quite clumpy straight from the pouch, so use clean hands to 'crumble' it into the pan to help to break it up if necessary, or use a wooden spoon to break it up as it heats through.)

5. Add the peas and the sauce, give everything a good stir and cook for 5–8 minutes until the rice is hot.

6. Serve with the cashew nuts sprinkled over.

SERVES 4

2 tsp sunflower oil
500g pork mince
4 tsp ginger purée (or fresh if you prefer)
2 garlic cloves, peeled and crushed
1 tsp Chinese 5-spice
200g baby corn, cut into 2cm pieces
2 x 250g microwave rice pouches
200g frozen peas

For the sauce
2 tbsp oyster sauce
4 tbsp dark soy sauce (I use reduced salt)
2 tbsp runny honey
2 tbsp water
1 lime, juiced

To Serve
75g cashew nuts, roughly chopped

SALMON WITH FETA & ORZO

25 MINS

This is a super simple way to cook salmon and adding crumbled feta on top is always going to be a win. The salty cheese works particularly well here with the oily fish. If you have children who are wary of big chunks of salmon, just break it up a little into the orzo before serving to them.

1. Heat the oil in a sauté pan over a medium heat and add the courgettes. Cook for 5 minutes or until just starting to soften.

2. Add the orzo, stock, spinach, pesto and plenty of salt and pepper. Give everything a good stir.

3. Sit the salmon fillets in the orzo (if they have skin on, place them in skin side up). Reduce the heat to low, put the lid on and cook for 10 minutes over a low heat.

4. Carefully flip the salmon over and give everything else a good stir (I actually find it easier here to remove the salmon briefly to a plate, stir the orzo well, then return the salmon to the pan).

5. Crumble over the feta cheese and put the lid back on. Cook for a further 5–10 minutes until everything is cooked through. Squeeze over the lemon juice and serve.

SERVES 4

2 tsp olive oil
2 courgettes, cut into 2cm cubes
300g orzo (uncooked)
800ml hot vegetable stock
    (made with a stock cube is fine)
150g baby spinach
2 tbsp green pesto
4 salmon fillets (about 500g in total)
100g feta cheese
1 lemon, halved
sea salt and freshly ground
    black pepper

WEEKEND TREATS

SLOW COOKER
CHOCOLATE PUDDLE PUDDING

1 HOUR 40 MINS

I've shared a few versions of this pudding before online, but this is the classic. My go-to slow cooker chocolate pudding complete with its own sauce. Don't be put off by the slightly unusual method: everything feels a little clumsy as you make it (water? over a cake?), but I promise it will all come good. I first learned about this method of pudding-cooking from an ancient Mary Berry book, where you cooked a lemon sponge in the oven that left a miraculous lemon custard at the bottom. This recipe works even better in a slow cooker than a traditional oven, as the slow cooking gently keeps the sauce at the bottom quite stable.

1. **Grease the slow cooker pot very well with the 20g room-temperature butter (see Notes).**

2. **In a large bowl, mix all the pudding ingredients together until smooth (use an electric whisk if you have one). Put into the greased slow cooker and smooth out.**

3. **In another small bowl, mix the sugar and cocoa powder for the topping. Sprinkle this evenly over the top of the pudding batter.**

4. **Carefully pour over the boiling water. (It will all look a bit odd at the moment, but keep the faith!)**

5. **Put the lid on the slow cooker and cook on HIGH for 1½ – 2½ hours, until the cake is firm in the middle. Serve immediately.**

SERVES 8

20g unsalted butter, at room temperature, for greasing

For the Pudding
100g unsalted butter, melted
250g self-raising flour
125g soft light brown sugar
30g cocoa powder
1 tsp baking powder
3 eggs
150ml milk (semi-skimmed or full-fat)
2 tsp vanilla extract
100g white chocolate chips

For the Topping
150g soft light brown sugar
25g cocoa powder
500ml boiling water

If your slow cooker is the ceramic type (and is NOT non-stick) I recommend lining it with baking paper before cooking this pudding. Just squash a large sheet into the shape of the cooker (so there are no gaps for the sauce to escape) and there will be no need to use the butter to grease it.

This recipe serves 8 as it's the right size for a 3.5 litre slow cooker. Keep leftovers in the fridge and re-heat in the microwave (or serve cold) for pudding the next day.

IF YOU DON'T HAVE A SLOW COOKER...
Bake at 160°C fan for 30–40 minutes.

SLOW COOKER
PEANUT BUTTER BLONDIES

55 MINS

If you've never tried a blondie before, they should be something like a brownie but not...brown! Here, the crunchy peanut butter gives them added flavour and texture. They are surprisingly easy to over-cook in a standard oven, so baking these in a slow cooker is particularly useful.

1. Mix the butter, sugar, peanut butter, eggs and plain flour in a bowl until well combined.

2. Grease the slow cooker pot with the 10g room-temperature butter (see Notes).

3. Spoon the blondie mixture into the pot, smooth the top and sprinkle over the nuts. Put a clean tea towel over the top of the slow cooker, then place the lid on top of that (this absorbs the water and stops the cake from being wet).

4. Cook on HIGH for 45 minutes–1 hour 15 minutes, or until the top of the blondies are evenly cooked and the mixture doesn't look wet in the middle.

5. Leave to cool, with the tea towel and lid removed, then turn out of the slow cooker and cut into pieces.

SERVES 8

10g unsalted butter, at room temperature, for greasing

For the Blondie Batter
125g unsalted butter, melted
150g soft light brown sugar
100g crunchy peanut butter
2 eggs
100g plain flour
60g salted peanuts, roughly chopped (or swap for chocolate chips if you prefer!)

If your slow cooker is the ceramic type (and is NOT non-stick) I recommend lining it with baking paper before cooking these blondies. Just squash a large sheet into the shape of the cooker (so there are no gaps for the batter to escape) and there will be no need to use the butter to grease it.

This recipe serves 8 as it's the right size for a 3.5-litre slow cooker. Keep leftovers in an airtight container for up to 5 days.

IF YOU DON'T HAVE A SLOW COOKER...
At step 3 above, pour the mixture into a 20 x 20cm cake tin, lined with baking paper. Bake in a preheated oven at 180°C fan/200°C/Gas Mark 6 for 15–25 minutes or until a skewer inserted into the middle comes out just clean. Do not overbake them or they will be dry.

CHOCO-NUT PINWHEELS

25 MINS

Sometimes the simplest ideas are the best, and that's true here. A nifty little rolling technique means that although these only take minutes to put together, they somehow look almost professional. They make a delicious afternoon treat or morning pastry.

1. Preheat the oven to 200°C fan/220°C/Gas Mark 7 and line a baking tray with baking paper (not greaseproof).

2. Unroll the puff pastry and spread the chocolate spread all over the surface.

3. Position a short end of the rectangle of pastry nearest you, then roll it up so that the spread is on the inside.

4. Use a sharp knife to cut the roll in half, in half again and so on until you end up with 8 equal-sized pieces. Wiping the knife between each cut will help to keep the swirls looking neat.

5. Place the pastries, swirl side up, on the lined baking tray and brush the tops and sides with the beaten egg.

6. Sprinkle a little of the chopped hazelnuts on top of each one and bake for 15–20 minutes or until golden all over.

SERVES 8

320g ready-rolled puff pastry
125g chocolate hazelnut spread
1 egg, beaten
30g hazelnuts, roughly chopped

This recipe makes 8 because of the size of the pastry sheet. Store the leftovers in an airtight container for up to 2 days.

PAIN AU CHOCOLAT BREAD & BUTTER PUDDING

3 HOURS 10 MINS / SERVE WITH VANILLA CRÈME FRAÎCHE

This recipe is the perfect solution for any pastries slightly past their best (you could use ordinary croissants instead, and add choc chips if you like). They are brought back to life in this comforting pudding. Cooking dairy in a slow cooker can be a little tricky as it can split, so the key is to cook this very gently on the low temperature. This is a brilliant recipe to prepare in advance, as the pastry soaks up the liquid more. Make up to step 3, cover and store in the fridge overnight for cooking the next day.

1. **Grease the slow cooker pot very well with the 20g room-temperature butter (see Notes).**

2. **Tip the cubes of pain au chocolat into the pot and sprinkle over the sugar.**

3. **Put the eggs, milk, double cream, cinnamon and vanilla in a jug or bowl and whisk until combined. Pour this over the pain au chocolat.**

4. **Put a clean tea towel over the top of the slow cooker, then place the lid on top of that (this absorbs the water and stops the pudding from being wet).**

5. **Cook on LOW for 3–4 hours until the top of the pudding is evenly cooked and doesn't look wet in the middle. Serve immediately.**

SERVES 8

20g unsalted butter, at room temperature, for greasing

For the Pudding
300g pain au chocolat, cut into 3cm cubes
50g soft light brown sugar
4 eggs
500ml milk (semi-skimmed or full-fat)
150ml double cream
2 tsp ground cinnamon
2 tsp vanilla extract

If your slow cooker is the ceramic type (and is NOT non-stick) I would recommend lining it with baking paper. Just squash a large sheet into the shape of the cooker (so there are no gaps for the pudding mixture to escape) and there will be no need to use the butter to grease it.

VANILLA CRÈME FRAÎCHE

5 MINS / SERVES 4

This quick mix is a good alternative to custard or ice cream.

200ml crème fraîche (reduced fat if you prefer)
2 tsp icing sugar, sifted
2 tsp vanilla extract

Mix the ingredients together in a bowl and serve.

This recipe serves 8 as it's the right size for a 3.5 litre slow cooker. Keep leftovers in the fridge and re-heat in the microwave (or serve cold) for pudding the next day.

VANILLA CRÈME FRAÎCHE →

IF YOU DON'T HAVE A SLOW COOKER...
At step 4, place the pudding in an oven preheated to 170°C fan/190°C/Gas Mark 5
and bake for 30–45 minutes or until the pudding is just set.

KITCHEN SINK POPCORN

15 MINS

So called because we add everything but the kitchen sink! Popcorn is surprisingly easy to make at home and is one of those things that really is so much better fresh from the pan. Add some treats here to make it even more special. Best served while watching your favourite family film, of course.

2 tbsp sunflower oil
100g popcorn kernels (the yellow, un-popped type)
200g milk chocolate, cut into small chunks
100g mini marshmallows
200g sugar-coated chocolates, such as Smarties or M&Ms
100g salted peanuts

1. **Heat the oil in a sauté pan over a medium heat and add the popcorn kernels. Put the lid on quickly!**

2. **Leave the lid on and wait for the popping to start. Once it starts, it will pop almost continuously for 5–10 minutes. During this time, carefully use a tea towel to hold the lid down and shake the pan once or twice.**

3. **When the popping slows down to only one pop every 4 or 5 seconds, turn off the heat.**

4. **Take off the lid, sprinkle in the chocolate chunks and marshmallows, put the lid back on, and – again – use a tea towel to hold the lid on the pan and give it a good shake.**

5. **Leave the lid on the pan and set aside for 5 minutes. Add the candied chocolates and the peanuts and give everything a good stir. Leave to cool.**

Any leftovers can be stored in a sealed tin for up to 5 days.

SLOW COOKER
BANOFFEE CAKE

I've probably made banana cake more than any other cake in the last 10 years. Please tell me I'm not the only one who has a continual stream of forgotten brown bananas passing through their fruit bowl?! This method of cooking a banana cake saves the challenge of trying not to overcook a deep loaf in a traditional oven, and the toffees melt to pockets of gooey caramel. The bananas need to be very ripe for this recipe: the darker and more spotty the skins are the better!

1. Grease the slow cooker pot very well with the 20g room-temperature butter (see Notes).

2. Mix all the cake batter ingredients together until smooth (use an electric hand-held whisk if you have one). Pour the batter into the slow cooker pot and smooth it out with the back of a spoon. Sit the toffees on top of the cake – there's no need to press them down.

3. Put a clean tea towel over the top of the slow cooker, then sit the lid on top of that (this absorbs the water and stops the cake from being wet).

4. Cook on HIGH for 2–3 hours until the top of the cake is evenly cooked and doesn't look wet in the middle.

5. Leave the cake to cool for 5–10 minutes, then carefully turn it out of the tin.

SERVES 8

20g unsalted butter, at room temperature
100g toffees, unwrapped (hard or chewy)

For the Cake Batter
125g unsalted butter, melted
150g soft light brown sugar
250g self-raising flour
3 very ripe bananas, peeled and mashed
3 eggs

If your slow cooker is the ceramic type (and is NOT non-stick) I would recommend lining it with baking paper. Just squash a large sheet into the shape of the cooker (so there are no gaps for the batter to escape) and there will be no need to use the butter to grease it.

This recipe serves 8 as it's the right size for a 3.5 litre slow cooker. Leftovers will keep in an airtight container for up to 5 days.

IF YOU DON'T HAVE A SLOW COOKER...
Bake in a 1lb loaf tin, lined with baking paper, in a preheated oven at 160°C fan/180°C/Gas Mark 4 for 45–60 minutes or until a skewer inserted into the middle comes out clean. (You will find that with this method the toffees sink to the bottom a little, but don't let that put you off as it creates a delicious toffee layer.)

LAZY FRUIT PIE

30 MINS

This is something like a French galette but is made using ready-made pastry as a shortcut. The trick of preheating the baking tray and then carefully lifting the pie onto it (using the baking paper that the pastry is packed on), helps to crisp the base as the pie cooks. It's always best when served with scoops of ice cream melting into the fruit.

1. Put a baking tray into the oven and preheat the oven to 200°C fan/220°C/Gas Mark 7.

2. Place the apples, raspberries, cornflour, cinnamon and 30g of the caster sugar in a large bowl and mix well until the fruit is coated.

3. Unroll the pastry sheet (leave it on the baking paper it comes out of the box on – see Notes).

4. Pile the fruit into the middle of the pastry, leaving an uncovered rim of about 5cm all the way around the edge. Fold this edge in over the fruit.

5. Brush the pastry that you can still see with the beaten egg and sprinkle the remaining 20g of sugar over the top.

6. Bake for 20–25 minutes until the pastry is golden and the fruit is soft.

SERVES 6

4 apples, peeled, core removed and thinly sliced
100g raspberries
25g cornflour
1 tsp ground cinnamon
50g caster sugar
320g ready-rolled shortcrust pastry
1 egg, beaten

If your pastry didn't come on a baking paper sheet, just roll it out onto one. Be sure to use baking paper or baking parchment, not greaseproof paper (as this can stick).

This recipe serves 6, just because of the size of a sheet of pastry. Cold leftovers, stored in the fridge, make an excellent breakfast.

SLOW COOKER
DOUBLE CHOCOLATE FUDGE

Strictly speaking, this is not real fudge as we are using a shortcut of a tin of condensed milk. This method is simple and reliable, and the end result, complete with chunky pieces of extra chocolate, is totally decadent. We put the chocolate chunks in the freezer for 30 minutes while the fudge is cooking, so that they are less likely to melt into it when we add them to the hot fudge. Clever trick, right?!

1. **Put the white chocolate chunks into the freezer and line a dish (see Notes) with baking paper (not greaseproof).**

2. **Put the milk chocolate and condensed milk into the slow cooker pot. Give everything a good stir and put the lid on.**

3. **Cook on LOW for 30 minutes, stirring very well every 10 minutes.**

4. **When the fudge is thick and smooth, switch off the heat and beat in the vanilla and 150g of the chocolate chunks from the freezer.**

5. **Pour into the lined dish, smooth out the top and sprinkle over the remaining chocolate chunks.**

6. **Refrigerate overnight to set, then cut into 36 chunks. If your fudge is sticky when you cut it, put the cut chunks back into the fridge on the baking paper, out of the tin for at least 1–2 hours. I find that putting them back in like this helps them to dry out a little. You can store this in the fridge for up to a week.**

MAKES 36 CHUNKS

200g white chocolate, cut into chunks (see Notes)
400g milk chocolate, broken into cubes
1 x 397g tin condensed milk
2 tsp vanilla extract

I like to pour this into a 1lb loaf tin for thick slices of fudge. For smaller pieces, any dish or tin about 20 x 20cm will work.

IF YOU DON'T HAVE A SLOW COOKER...

Microwave: Put the milk chocolate and condensed milk into a large bowl and microwave for 1 minute. Mix very well, even if it looks like it doesn't need it! Repeat the cooking and mixing once or twice until the mixture is very smooth. Continue from step 3 above.

Hob: Put the milk chocolate and condensed milk into a large heatproof bowl over a saucepan of simmering water, over a low heat on the hob. Don't let the water touch the bottom of the bowl – it should be just the steam heating the bowl. Stir gently until everything is melted. Continue from step 3 above.

SLOW COOKER
PEAR & CHOCOLATE CRUMBLE

3 HOURS 40 MINS

Is this crumble exactly like the crunchy-topped texture of a traditional oven-baked crumble? No. Does the fruit cook slowly, to a sticky, jammy treat with a delicious cakey crumble top? Yes! You can easily make the crumble mixture in a mini food processor, but I do think the texture is slightly better if you make it by hand – I promise it only takes 5 minutes!

1. Peel the pears and cut each one into 3 evenly-sized pieces. (If they have seeds, scoop them out with a teaspoon.)

2. Put the pears into the bottom of the slow cooker and sprinkle with the sugar and cinnamon, then scatter the chocolate chips over the top.

3. Put the flour and butter into a small bowl and, using clean hands, rub the butter in by putting both hands into the bowl and lifting up some butter cubes with some of the flour and rubbing the mixture between your fingertips, letting the mixture fall through back down into the bowl. Repeat until the mixture looks like damp, lumpy sand!

4. Stir the sugar into the crumble mixture and sprinkle it over the pears. Sprinkle the oats on top.

5. Put a clean tea towel over the top of the slow cooker, then sit the lid on top of that (this absorbs any condensation). Cook on HIGH for 3 hours.

6. After the cooking time, remove the tea towel and put the lid back on the slow cooker, but sit it on the cooker ajar, so the moisture can escape. Cook for 30 minutes on HIGH to allow the crumble mixture to firm up.

SERVES 8

For the Fruit Mixture
750g pears (about 6)
40g caster sugar
1 tsp ground cinnamon
50g milk chocolate chips

For the Crumble Topping
175g plain flour
100g unsalted butter, cold, cut into small cubes
100g caster sugar
25g jumbo oats

This is best made in a smaller slow cooker if you have one: as it gives a deeper fruit layer. If you only have a large (say 6.5 litre) slow cooker, you may want to make double the recipe and freeze the rest for another day.

I used jumbo oats for texture, but regular oats would be fine too.

IF YOU DON'T HAVE A SLOW COOKER...

At step 5 above, put the crumble, uncovered, in the oven, preheated to 180°C fan/200°C/Gas Mark 6 for 30–40 minutes until the fruit is softened.

SLOW COOKER
RASPBERRY BAKEWELL CAKE

1 HOUR 10 MINS

I've fallen so deeply in love with this cake that I am now over the moon when I stumble on a leftover jar of jam in our fridge, just to have an excuse to make it. The ground almonds and gentle slow cooking give it a tender crumb that's ideal for an afternoon treat or served warm with ice cream.

1. Grease the slow cooker pot very well with the 20g room-temperature butter (see Notes).

2. Mix all the cake batter ingredients together in a bowl until smooth (use an electric whisk if you have one). Spoon into the greased slow cooker pot.

3. Dollop the jam into the sponge batter in small spoonfuls and swirl them in with a knife. Sprinkle the flaked almonds on top if you're using them.

4. Put a clean tea towel over the top of the slow cooker (this absorbs the water and stops the cake from being wet), then sit the lid on top of that.

5. Cook on HIGH for 1–2 hours or LOW for 2–3 hours until the top of the cake is evenly cooked and doesn't look wet in the middle.

6. Leave the cake to cool for 5–10 minutes, then carefully turn it out of the tin.

SERVES 8

20g unsalted butter, at room temperature, for greasing
150g raspberry jam
25g flaked almonds (optional)

For the Cake Batter
175g unsalted butter, at room temperature
175g caster sugar
175g self-raising flour
3 eggs
75g ground almonds
75ml milk (semi-skimmed or whole)

If your slow cooker is the ceramic type (and is NOT non-stick) I would recommend lining it with baking paper. Just squash a large sheet into the shape of the cooker (so there are no gaps for the cake batter to escape) and there will be no need to use the butter to grease it.

This recipe serves 8 as it's the right size for a 3.5 litre slow cooker. Leftovers will keep for up to 3 days in an airtight container.

IF YOU DON'T HAVE A SLOW COOKER...
Spoon the mixture into a 1lb loaf tin, lined with baking paper, finish as in step 3 above and bake in a preheated oven at 160°C fan/180°C/Gas Mark 4 for 45–60 minutes or until a skewer inserted into the middle comes out clean.

WEEKEND TREATS

NUTRITIONAL INFORMATION

Please use the nutritional information here as an approximate guide only. If you need exact measurements please confirm using your own branded ingredients. All measurements are per serving (as per the recipe page).

WEEKEND BREAKFASTS

PEANUT BUTTER GRANOLA
(Per Serving)
Kcals: 441
Protein: 14.5g
Fat: 24.0g
Sat fat: 5.8g
Carbs: 38.5g
Sugar: 17.7g
Fibre: 6.2g
Salt: 0.38g
32

CHOCOLATE CHERRY GRANOLA
(Per Serving)
Kcals: 140
Protein: 3.0g
Fat: 3.2g
Sat fat: 1.4g
Carbs: 23.9g
Sugars: 13.5g
Fibre: 2.0g
Salt: 0.05g
34

MAPLE PECAN GRANOLA
(Per Serving)
Kcals: 250
Protein: 6.0g
Fat: 11.2g
Sat fat: 1.1g
Carbs: 29.2g
Sugar: 9.0g
Fibre: 4.7g
Salt: 0.05g
35

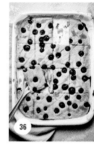

ONE-PAN PANCAKES
(Per Serving)
Kcals: 356
Protein: 9.6g
Fat: 10.3g
Sat fat: 2.1g
Carbs: 52.9g
Sugar: 16.7g
Fibre: 2.6g
Salt: 0.87
36

CHEESE & BACON STRATA
(Per Serving)
Kcals: 564
Protein: 35.7g
Carbs: 42g
Sugar: 10.8g
Fat: 27.3g
Sat fat: 11.7g
Fibre: 3.5g
Salt: 3.19g
38

CHORIZO HASH TRAYBAKE
(Per Serving)
Kcals: 586
Protein: 29.6g
Fat: 25.3g
Sat fat: 8.5g
Carbs: 56.3g
Sugar: 7.4g
Fibre: 7.4g
Salt: 2.44g
40

EASY CHEESY BREAKFAST BURRITOS
(Per Serving)
Kcals: 756
Protein: 34.0g
Fat: 49.0g
Sat fat: 19.3g
Carbs: 41.8g
Sugar: 6.0g
Fibre: 6.0g
Salt: 2.99g
42

ROASTED HONEY-GLAZED PLUMS
(Per Serving)
Kcals: 189
Protein: 3.2g
Carbs: 37.4g
Sugar: 28.2g
Fat: 2.2g
Sat fat: 0.3g
Fibre: 3.7g
Salt: 0.02
44

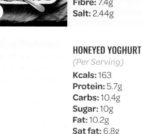

HONEYED YOGHURT
(Per Serving)
Kcals: 163
Protein: 5.7g
Carbs: 10.4g
Sugar: 10g
Fat: 10.2g
Sat fat: 6.8g
Fibre: 0.3g
Salt: 0.17g

44

DUTCH BABY
(Per Serving)
Kcals: 276
Protein: 12.1g
Fat: 10.6g
Sat fat: 2.7g
Carbs: 32.8g
Sugar: 18.2g
Fibre: 0.8g
Salt: 0.31g
46

MANGO SALAD
(Per Serving)
Kcals: 52
Protein: 1.0g
Fat: 0.4g
Sat fat: 0.1g
Carbs: 9.6g
Sugar: 9.3g
Fibre: 1.0g
Salt: 0.01g

46

YOGHURT BREAKFAST BARK
(Per Serving)
Kcals: 435
Protein: 11.9g
Carbs: 55.3g
Sugar: 35.6g
Fat: 17.2g
Sat fat: 9.1g
Fibre: 5.0g
Salt: 0.22g

18

MEAT-FREE MEALS

PANEER TIKKA ONE-POT
(Per Serving)
Kcals: 624
Protein: 29.2g
Fat: 27.9g
Sat fat: 10.4g
Carbs: 57.5g
Sugar: 10.0g
Fibre: 11.6g
Salt: 1.68g

52

MOROCCAN-STYLE AUBERGINE WITH APRICOTS
(Per Serving)
Kcals: 389
Protein: 13.2g
Fat: 11.5g
Sat fat: 1.6g
Carbs: 47.3g
Sugar: 24.8g
Fibre: 17.0g
Salt: 1.16g

54

CREAMY VEGETABLE CURRY
(Per Serving)
Kcals: 485
Protein: 17.0g
Fat: 16.4g
Sat fat: 7.2g
Carbs: 62.0g
Sugar: 26.7g
Fibre: 8.9g
Salt: 0.98g

56

CRISPY BUTTERNUT SQUASH & FETA PIE
(Per Serving)
Kcals: 570
Protein: 18.2g
Fat: 24.5g
Sat fat: 5.4g
Carbs: 62.1g
Sugar: 12.9g
Fibre: 9.5g
Salt: 1.25g

58

MEAT-FREE MONDAY TACOS
(Per Serving)
Kcals: 825
Protein: 36.9g
Fat: 39.3g
Sat fat: 12.0g
Carbs: 74.4g
Sugar: 18.0g
Fibre: 7.8g
Salt: 2.84g

60

FETA COUSCOUS
(Per Serving)
Kcals: 429
Protein: 14.9g
Fat: 14.2g
Sat fat: 4.8g
Carbs: 58.8g
Sugar: 2.5g
Fibre: 3.7g
Salt: 1.72g

62

PINK ONIONS
(Per Serving)
Kcals: 33
Protein: 0.4g
Fat: 0.0g
Sat fat: 0.0g
Carbs: 6.1g
Sugar: 5.4g
Fibre: 0.8g
Salt: 1.44g

62

JEWELLED SALAD
(Per Serving)
Kcals: 121
Protein: 1.5g
Fat: 3.7g
Sat fat: 0.5g
Carbs: 17.6g
Sugar: 17.0g
Fibre: 3.9g
Salt: 0.81g

63

SWEET POTATO & QUINOA CHILLI
(Per Serving)
Kcals: 467
Protein: 17.8g
Fat: 4.6g
Sat fat: 0.8g
Carbs: 80.2g
Sugar: 24.7g
Fibre: 16.4g
Salt: 1.70g

64

NUTRITIONAL INFORMATION

NACHO LOADED FRIES
(Per Serving)
Kcals: 708
Protein: 24.4g
Fat: 33.1g
Sat fat: 8.1g
Carbs: 69.9g
Sugar: 9.4g
Fibre: 11.2g
Salt: 1.17g

66

SNEAKY VEG MAC & CHEESE
(Per Serving)
Kcals: 601
Protein: 28.4g
Fat: 25.7g
Sat fat: 14.4g
Carbs: 62.1g
Sugar: 7.4g
Fibre: 3.1g
Salt: 3.33g

68

HALLOUMI FAJITA-STYLE TRAYBAKE
(Per Serving)
Kcals: 573
Protein: 20.4g
Fat: 31.7g
Sat fat: 16.2g
Carbs: 48.7g
Sugar: 10.8g
Fibre: 5.4g
Salt: 1.78g

70

PILES OF PASTA

CHICKEN CACCIATORE PASTA
(Per Serving)
Kcals: 722
Protein: 70.7g
Fat: 22.3g
Sat fat: 9.4g
Carbs: 55.8g
Sugar: 12.5g
Fibre: 7.7g
Salt: 3.88g

74

CREAMY GNOCCHI TRAYBAKE
(Per Serving)
Kcals: 555
Protein: 19.4g
Fat: 22.2g
Sat fat: 12.3g
Carbs: 66.7g
Sugar: 15.3g
Fibre: 3.8g
Salt: 1.80g

76

SPANAKOPITA-STYLE PASTA
(Per Serving)
Kcals: 529
Protein: 22.1g
Fat: 23.2g
Sat fat: 13.6g
Carbs: 55.5g
Sugar: 3.4g
Fibre: 4.9g
Salt: 3.13g

78

SAUSAGE GNOCCHI
(Per Serving)
Kcals: 794
Protein: 30.4g
Fat: 32.0g
Sat fat: 11.2g
Carbs: 89.2g
Sugar: 23.2g
Fibre: 16.1g
Salt: 3.19g

80

ONE-PAN LASAGNE
(Per Serving)
Kcals: 657
Protein: 50.4g
Fat: 19.1g
Sat fat: 10.7g
Carbs: 67.1g
Sugar: 22.0g
Fibre: 7.6g
Salt: 2.44g

82

MEAT FEAST PIZZA PASTA
(Per Serving)
Kcals: 624
Protein: 32.2g
Fat: 30.4g
Sat fat: 13.2g
Carbs: 52.2g
Sugar: 9.1g
Fibre: 6.1g
Salt: 4.27g

84

MUSHROOM ORZOTTO
(Per Serving)
Kcals: 452
Protein: 22.1g
Fat: 14.5g
Sat fat: 7.8g
Carbs: 56.1g
Sugar: 4.6g
Fibre: 4.8g
Salt: 2.85g

86

SALMON PRIMAVERA PASTA
(Per Serving)
Kcals: 582
Protein: 31.3g
Fat: 22.5g
Sat fat: 7.7g
Carbs: 59.7g
Sugar: 6.5g
Fibre: 7.8g
Salt: 3.29g

88

CREAMY BROCCOLI & BEEF TORTELLINI
(Per Serving)
Kcals: 691
Protein: 54.4g
Fat: 27.3g
Sat fat: 13.4g
Carbs: 54.2g
Sugar: 11.1g
Fibre: 5.0g
Salt: 1.63g

90

ITALIAN-STYLE BRAISED BEEF WITH ORZO
(Per Serving)
Kcals: 587
Protein: 42.3g
Fat: 22.1g
Sat fat: 10.0g
Carbs: 50.9g
Sugar: 15.9g
Fibre: 6.9g
Salt: 1.79g

92

GREMOLATA
(Per Serving)
Kcals: 4
Protein: 0.3g
Fat: 0.1g
Sat fat: 0.0g
Carbs: 0.3g
Sugar: 0.0g
Fibre: 0.3g
Salt: 0.01g

92

CAPRESE PASTA
(Per Serving)
Kcals: 526
Protein: 21.8g
Fat: 17.6g
Sat fat: 6.3g
Carbs: 66.1g
Sugar: 14.5g
Fibre: 6.9g
Salt: 2.29g

94

BAKES & BREADS

CUMIN-CRUSTED LAMB BAKE
(Per 628g)
Kcals: 640
Protein: 38.9g
Fat: 30.3g
Sat fat: 12.1g
Carbs: 49.3g
Sugar: 7.0g
Fibre: 7.9g
Salt: 0.46g

98

PESTO ROAST PORK
(Per Serving)
Kcals: 486
Protein: 39.0g
Fat: 22.2g
Sat fat: 5.4g
Carbs: 30.1g
Sugar: 2.4g
Fibre: 4.7g
Salt: 1.74g

100

STICKY GINGER PULLED HAM
(Per Serving)
Kcals: 518
Protein: 37.7g
Fat: 15.3g
Sat fat: 5.0g
Carbs: 53.9g
Sugar: 33.2g
Fibre: 1.8g
Salt: 4.58g

102

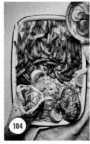

OREGANO & LEMON CHICKEN WRAPS
(Per Serving)
Kcals: 901
Protein: 60.8g
Fat: 28.3g
Sat fat: 5.9g
Carbs: 110.4g
Sugar: 11.2g
Fibre: 10.7g
Salt: 1.93g

104

SAUSAGE PUFF PIE
(Per Serving)
Kcals: 968
Protein: 28.3g
Fat: 54.5g
Sat fat: 21.5g
Carbs: 83.8g
Sugar: 23.8g
Fibre: 15.0g
Salt: 3.95g

106

CHICKEN & FETA TRAYBAKE
(Per Serving)
Kcals: 711
Protein: 51.5g
Fat: 35.7g
Sat fat: 10.9g
Carbs: 42.7g
Sugar: 11.0g
Fibre: 8.7g
Salt: 1.29g

108

STICKY PORK MEATBALLS
(Per Serving)
Kcals: 569
Protein: 39.2g
Fat: 16.5g
Sat fat: 5.2g
Carbs: 62.2g
Sugar: 18.2g
Fibre: 5.0g
Salt: 2.92g

110

NUTRITIONAL INFORMATION

COOLING CUCUMBER SALAD
(Per Serving)
Kcals: 57
Protein: 3.8g
Fat: 2.1g
Sat fat: 1.1g
Carbs: 5.2g
Sugar: 4.9g
Fibre: 0.7g
Salt: 0.83g
112

RED SLAW
(Per Serving)
Kcals: 222
Protein: 2.1g
Fat: 14.5g
Sat fat: 1.7g
Carbs: 17.9g
Sugar: 16.3g
Fibre: 5.4g
Salt: 0.79g
112

PINEAPPLE CRUNCH SALAD
(Per Serving)
Kcals: 109
Protein: 2.4g
Fat: 0.4g
Sat fat: 0.0g
Carbs: 20.9g
Sugar: 20.6g
Fibre: 6.0g
Salt: 0.35g
113

BEEF & MUSHROOM POT PIE
(Per Serving)
Kcals: 833
Protein: 44.0g
Fat: 39.4g
Sat fat: 12.7g
Carbs: 71.2g
Sugar: 11.6g
Fibre: 9.4g
Salt: 3.08g
114

CAJUN-STYLE PRAWN TRAYBAKE
(Per Serving)
Kcals: 362
Protein: 23.2g
Fat: 5.3g
Sat fat: 0.9g
Carbs: 52.0g
Sugar: 10.8g
Fibre: 6.7g
Salt: 1.11g
116

BRAISED BEEF TACOS
(Per Serving)
Kcals: 767
Protein: 66.4g
Fat: 37.5g
Sat fat: 13.7g
Carbs: 38.8g
Sugar: 6.5g
Fibre: 4.8g
Salt: 3.57g
118

FISHERMAN'S BAKE
(Per Serving)
Kcals: 828
Protein: 37.0g
Fat: 41.0g
Sat fat: 23.3g
Carbs: 73.9g
Sugar: 14.8g
Fibre: 8.3g
Salt: 0.89g
120

CHICKEN TIKKA-STYLE TRAYBAKE
(Per Serving)
Kcals: 712
Protein: 49.9g
Fat: 31.8g
Sat fat: 6.8g
Carbs: 54.8g
Sugar: 16.4g
Fibre: 8.0g
Salt: 2.38g
122

COMFORT FOOD

CHICKEN TACO SOUP
(Per Serving)
Kcals: 518
Protein: 35.0g
Fat: 18.8g
Sat fat: 6.6g
Carbs: 46.7g
Sugar: 18.1g
Fibre: 10.8g
Salt: 2.16g
126

BACON & LENTIL SOUP
(Per Serving)
Kcals: 377
Protein: 25.3g
Fat: 13.9g
Sat fat: 4.5g
Carbs: 31.5g
Sugar: 6.5g
Fibre: 11.7g
Salt: 3.74g
128

CHICKEN STEW WITH PARMESAN DUMPLINGS
(Per Serving)
Kcals: 976
Protein: 57.3g
Fat: 51.2g
Sat fat: 22.8g
Carbs: 67.9g
Sugar: 7.0g
Fibre: 9.2g
Salt: 3.54g
130

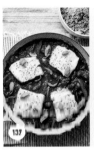

HOT-HEADED COD
(Per Serving)

Kcals: 245
Protein: 25.6g
Fat: 8.2g
Sat fat: 1.3g
Carbs: 15.0g
Sugar: 13.7g
Fibre: 1.7g
Salt: 0.47g

137

LAMB & SPINACH CURRY
(Per Serving)

Kcals: 533
Protein: 36.5g
Fat: 24.7g
Sat fat: 7.1g
Carbs: 35.1g
Sugar: 22.2g
Fibre: 10.2g
Salt: 5.03g

134

TOMATO & ONION SALAD
(Per Serving)

Kcals: 29
Protein: 0.9g
Fat: 0.1g
Sat fat: 0.0g
Carbs: 5.1g
Sugar: 4.8g
Fibre: 1.7g
Salt: 0.72g

134

BBQ SAUSAGE & BEAN BAKE
(Per Serving)

Kcals: 751
Protein: 21.6g
Fat: 33.7g
Sat fat: 11.1g
Carbs: 82.9g
Sugar: 31.4g
Fibre: 17.3g
Salt: 1.98g

136

MINTED LAMB STEW
(Per Serving)

Kcals: 549
Protein: 40.3g
Fat: 20.0g
Sat fat: 9.1g
Carbs: 52.1g
Sugar: 15.0g
Fibre: 7.2g
Salt: 1.96g

138

TURKEY TACO RICE
(Per Serving)

Kcals: 496
Protein: 43.6g
Fat: 7.3g
Sat fat: 1.5g
Carbs: 59.8g
Sugar: 9.9g
Fibre: 8.3g
Salt: 2.31g

140

RED CURRY CHICKEN NOODLE SOUP
(Per Serving)

Kcals: 661
Protein: 36.8g
Fat: 21.8g
Sat fat: 9.3g
Carbs: 51.8g
Sugar: 6.6g
Fibre: 3g
Salt: 3.44g

142

PORK LETTUCE CUPS
(Per Serving)

Kcals: 453
Protein: 33.4g
Fat: 13.4g
Sat fat: 4.8g
Carbs: 49.0g
Sugar: 7.4g
Fibre: 3.8g
Salt: 4.72g

144

PEANUT DIPPING SAUCE
(Per Serving)

Kcals: 140
Protein: 5.4g
Fat: 10.5g
Sat fat: 2.6g
Carbs: 5.2g
Sugar: 4.0g
Fibre: 1.4g
Salt: 0.89g

146

LEMON COUSCOUS
(Per Serving)

Kcals: 320
Protein: 11.0g
Fat: 4.4g
Sat fat: 0.7g
Carbs: 58.9g
Sugar: 2.4g
Fibre: 3.4g
Salt: 1.11g

146

CORONATION COUSCOUS
(Per Serving)

Kcals: 473
Protein: 16.4g
Fat: 12.7g
Sat fat: 1.5g
Carbs: 69.5g
Sugar: 11.0g
Fibre: 7.4g
Salt: 0.93g

147

SPOONFUL SALAD
(Per Serving)

Kcals: 111
Protein: 2.7g
Fat: 7.6g
Sat fat: 1.1g
Carbs: 5.1g
Sugar: 4.8g
Fibre: 4.4g
Salt: 0.40g

147

NUTRITIONAL INFORMATION

PORK CHILLI
(Per Serving)
Kcals: 617
Protein: 87.1g
Fat: 17.3g
Sat fat: 5.6g
Carbs: 24.5g
Sugar: 13.6g
Fibre: 7.1g
Salt: 1.24g

148

148

SPICY CORN SALAD
(Per Serving)
Kcals: 101
Protein: 2.2g
Fat: 4.8g
Sat fat: 0.7g
Carbs: 11.0g
Sugar: 6.5g
Fibre: 2.6g
Salt: 0.36g

UPSIDE-DOWN LOADED NACHOS
(Per Serving)
Kcals: 636
Protein: 45.3g
Fat: 19.1g
Sat fat: 7.1g
Carbs: 64.5g
Sugar: 11.5g
Fibre: 12.6g
Salt: 1.93g

150

HONEY & MUSTARD PORK
(Per Serving)
Kcals: 458
Protein: 34.8g
Fat: 10.0g
Sat fat: 3.5g
Carbs: 52.7g
Sugar: 20.3g
Fibre: 9.0g
Salt: 1.47g

152

CHORIZO & BEAN STEW
(Per Serving)
Kcals: 487
Protein: 27.0g
Fat: 19.3g
Sat fat: 6.6g
Carbs: 41.4g
Sugar: 18.2g
Fibre: 19.1g
Salt: 3.12g

153

SPANISH-ISH CHICKEN & CHORIZO RICE
(Per Serving)
Kcals: 769
Protein: 50.9g
Fat: 34.6g
Sat fat: 11.1g
Carbs: 58.3g
Sugar: 14.2g
Fibre: 11.8g
Salt: 3.93g

154

SPICED ROAST CHICKEN
(Per Serving)
Kcals: 636
Protein: 47.5g
Fat: 48.3g
Sat fat: 11.1g
Carbs: 1.9g
Sugar: 0.3g
Fibre: 0.9g
Salt: 0.43g

156

SMOKY RED FRITTATA
(Per Serving)
Kcals: 489
Protein: 30.7g
Fat: 26.0g
Sat fat: 8.7g
Carbs: 30.0g
Sugar: 6.9g
Fibre: 6.5g
Salt: 2.31g

158

SATAY-STYLE BRAISED BEEF
(Per Serving)
Kcals: 455
Protein: 47.7g
Fat: 21.1g
Sat fat: 10.6g
Carbs: 16.9g
Sugar: 6.5g
Fibre: 3.4g
Salt: 2.64g

160

SPEEDY SUPPERS

THAI-STYLE RED RICE
(Per Serving)
Kcals: 521
Protein: 34.8g
Fat: 19.7g
Sat fat: 9.4g
Carbs: 48.5g
Sugar: 5.9g
Fibre: 5.7g
Salt: 1.88g

164

PRAWN & PEA ORZO
(Per Serving)
Kcals: 540
Protein: 31.1g
Fat: 20.7g
Sat fat: 10.6g
Carbs: 53.8g
Sugar: 7.6g
Fibre: 7.2g
Salt: 2.50g

166

FANCY FISH FINGER SANDWICHES
(Per Serving)
Kcals: 525
Protein: 33.8g
Fat: 26.4g
Sat fat: 8.4g
Carbs: 36.0g
Sugar: 4.1g
Fibre: 2.9g
Salt: 1.81g

168

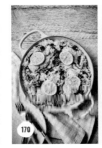

ZESTY CHICKEN PILAF
(Per Serving)
Kcals: 439
Protein: 46.0g
Fat: 6.8g
Sat fat: 1.4g
Carbs: 45.6g
Sugar: 1.0g
Fibre: 3.0g
Salt: 1.02g

170

TRAFFIC-LIGHT PIZZA
(Per Serving)
Kcals: 665
Protein: 25.4g
Fat: 23.6g
Sat fat: 14.3g
Carbs: 84.5g
Sugar: 11.7g
Fibre: 6.0g
Salt: 3.15g

172

SPEEDY AVOCADO SALSA
(Per Serving)
Kcals: 173
Protein: 1.8g
Fat: 16.7g
Sat fat: 3.6g
Carbs: 2.6g
Sugar: 1.7g
Fibre: 2.8g
Salt: 0.14g

174

CAESAR-ISH SALAD
(Per Serving)
Kcals: 253
Protein: 6.7g
Fat: 23.0g
Sat fat: 3.8g
Carbs: 2.8g
Sugar: 2.7g
Fibre: 3.4g
Salt: 0.47g

174

SESAME & GINGER SLAW
(Per Serving)
Kcals: 254
Protein: 3.3g
Fat: 16.7g
Sat fat: 2.5g
Carbs: 19.2g
Sugar: 18.4g
Fibre: 5.7g
Salt: 0.75g

175

MINTED PEA SALAD
(Per Serving)
Kcals: 187
Protein: 8.0g
Fat: 12.5g
Sat fat: 4.5g
Carbs: 8.4g
Sugar: 4.8g
Fibre: 4.4g
Salt: 0.78g

175

TURKEY & LIME BURGERS
(Per Serving)
Kcals: 522
Protein: 41.9g
Fat: 19.9g
Sat fat: 3.5g
Carbs: 42.0g
Sugar: 12.0g
Fibre: 3.9g
Salt: 1.01g

176

POLLO PESTO RICE
(Per Serving)
Kcals: 644
Protein: 55.4g
Fat: 23.0g
Sat fat: 7.3g
Carbs: 49.3g
Sugar: 6.4g
Fibre: 4.8g
Salt: 2.85g

178

CHEESY BEAN TORTILLA ROLLS
(Per Serving)
Kcals: 816
Protein: 32.1g
Fat: 34.9g
Sat fat: 13.1g
Carbs: 86.8g
Sugar: 11.7g
Fibre: 14.1g
Salt: 3.57g

180

SPEEDY GINGER PORK STIR-FRY
(Per Serving)
Kcals: 615
Protein: 36.3g
Fat: 25.0g
Sat fat: 6.8g
Carbs: 58.7g
Sugar: 16.1g
Fibre: 5.3g
Salt: 3.34g

182

SALMON WITH FETA & ORZO
(Per Serving)
Kcals: 708
Protein: 43.4g
Fat: 33.3g
Sat fat: 8.7g
Carbs: 55.9g
Sugar: 5.4g
Fibre: 5.6g
Salt: 3.08g

184

NUTRITIONAL INFORMATION

WEEKEND TREATS

CHOCOLATE PUDDLE PUDDING
(Per Serving)
Kcals: 489
Protein: 9.1g
Fat: 20.4g
Sat fat: 11.9g
Carbs: 64.7g
Sugar: 41.3g
Fibre: 3.5g
Salt: 0.58g

188

PEANUT BUTTER BLONDIES
(Per Serving)
Kcals: 389
Protein: 8.8g
Fat: 25.7g
Sat fat: 10.9g
Carbs: 29.7g
Sugar: 19.7g
Fibre: 2.1g
Salt: 0.16g

190

CHOCO-NUT PINWHEELS
(Per Wheel)
Kcals: 279
Protein: 5.0g
Fat: 18.8g
Sat fat: 6.9g
Carbs: 21.5g
Sugar: 9.6g
Fibre: 1.9g
Salt: 0.39g

192

PAIN AU CHOCOLAT BREAD & BUTTER PUD
(Per Serving)
Kcals: 351
Protein: 8.8g
Fat: 22.2g
Sat fat: 11.5g
Carbs: 27.5g
Sugar: 15.8g
Fibre: 1.4g
Salt: 0.42g

194

VANILLA CRÈME FRAÎCHE
(Per Serving)
Kcals: 203
Protein: 1.1g
Fat: 20.2g
Sat fat: 13.7g
Carbs: 2.9g
Sugar: 2.7g
Fibre: 0.0g
Salt: 0.03g

194

KITCHEN SINK POPCORN
(Per Serving)
Kcals: 421
Protein: 8.5g
Fat: 20.3g
Sat fat: 8.7g
Carbs: 49.4g
Sugar: 38.9g
Fibre: 3.2g
Salt: 0.26g

196

BANOFFEE CAKE
(Per Serving)
Kcals: 433
Protein: 7.1g
Fat: 19.7g
Sat fat: 11.3g
Carbs: 55.9g
Sugar: 29.9g
Fibre: 1.8g
Salt: 0.48g

198

LAZY FRUIT PIE
(Per Serving)
Kcals: 350
Protein: 5.4g
Fat: 18.2g
Sat fat: 6.6g
Carbs: 39.6g
Sugar: 17.3g
Fibre: 3.5g
Salt: 0.35g

200

DOUBLE CHOCOLATE FUDGE
(Per Serving)
Kcals: 125
Protein: 2.1g
Fat: 6.1g
Sat fat: 3.7g
Carbs: 15.1g
Sugar: 15.1g
Fibre: 0.3g
Salt: 0.08g

202

PEAR & CHOCOLATE CRUMBLE
(Per Serving)
Kcals: 335
Protein: 3.2g
Fat: 12.6g
Sat fat: 7.7g
Carbs: 49.9g
Sugar: 31.9g
Fibre: 4.3g
Salt: 0.01g

204

RASPBERRY BAKEWELL CAKE
(Per Serving)
Kcals: 486
Protein: 7.9g
Fat: 27.8g
Sat fat: 13.9g
Carbs: 49.7g
Sugar: 33.7g
Fibre: 2.7g
Salt: 0.29g

206

INDEX

INDEX

INDEX

ACKNOWLEDGEMENTS

As always, the biggest thank you goes to all of YOU. If you've used my recipes, clicked on my website or followed me on social media – THANK YOU! Thank you for sharing your food struggles with me so I can try and come up with recipes that help and that genuinely make your life a little easier. I hope this book helps smooth the juggles of family life.

Lydia and the Harper Collins team – Thank you all for making another vision come to life. We have made a second beautiful book – woohoo! Thank you to everyone who has been involved from the initial concept, for the meticulous editing, the beautiful visuals and of course the sales teams behind the scenes. George and Sim, thank you for all your planning and brilliant work. Lydia, as always you've been so wonderful to work with. THANK YOU!

Sam, Giz, Pippa and Emma – Thank you for being an absolute dream team to work with. You are all a total inspiration. PS Please can we photoshop my wrinkles out next time, thanks.

Laurie – What a stroke of luck to have an agent who not only cares as much as I do, but is also an all-round gem of a person. Thank you for all your hard work.

Anna – As always, you deserve so much credit for this book. How could I do it without you? You've kept me going and reminded me why doing this work matters so much. I'm forever indebted to you and so grateful for you as my confidant and colleague.

Zoë – You somehow manage to be my village, even from the other end of the country. I value you and our daily ramblings more than you can know.

Deirdre – Thank you for everything, I'm so grateful for the lasting impact of our work.

Debbie – Thank you as always for your endless testing and feedback, especially on my tight deadlines. You are the only person who would send me a recipe review when you've just landed from a sky dive!

Claire and Miranda – Thank you so much as always for being on the Taming Twins team. Your work has allowed me the time and space to write these books, which wouldn't have been possible otherwise.

Emma – Dog-walk morning chats have got me through another book! Thank you for helping me try to understand our job and making me laugh such a lot in the process.

Imogen, Hattie, Hugo and Sophia – The support and enthusiasm from you all for this job I do has meant the world. So lucky to have you all in my life. (Extra mention to Hattie – THANK YOU for the testing, you were amazing!)

Dem – Thank you for loving me so fiercely, even when I am writing a book, knee-deep in slow cookers and hard work to live with! I am forever in awe of how you juggle so much, make it appear effortless and still find time to support me in every one of my own endeavours. Thank you, thank you, thank you.

George and Harriet – Thank you for your reviews, your love, your support and just astounding me every day with what amazing people you are. You inspire me to be the best I can be.